A 10

BSA A7 & A10 TWINS

Owen Wright

CONTENTS

FOREWORD	4
HISTORY	5
EVOLUTION	10
SPECIFICATION	13
ROAD TESTS	22
OWNER'S VIEW	29
BUYING	32
CLUBS, SPECIALISTS & BOOKS	34
PHOTO GALLERY	36

ISBN 0 85429 446 5

A FOULIS Motorcycling Book

First published 1984

© Haynes Publishing Group

All rights reserved. No part of this book may be reproduced or transmitted in any form or by any means, electronic or mechanical, including photocopying, recording or by any information storage or retrieval system, without written permission from the publisher.

Published by:
Haynes Publishing Group
Sparkford, Yeovil,
Somerset BA22 7JJ

Distributed in USA by:
Haynes Publications Inc.
861 Lawrence Drive, Newbury Park, California 91320, USA

Cover design: Rowland Smith
Page Layout: Teresa Woodside
Photographs: Andrew Morland and Author
Road tests: The Motor Cycle and Motor Cycling, courtesy of EMAP
Printed in England by: J.H. Haynes & Co. Ltd

Titles in the Super Profile series

Ariel Square Four (F388)
BMW R69 & R69/S (F387)
Brough Superior SS100 (F364)
BSA Bantam (F333)
Honda CB750 sohc (F351)
MV Agusta America (F334)
Norton Commando (F335)
Sunbeam S7 & S8 (F363)
Triumph Thunderbird (F353)
Triumph Trident (F352)
KSS Velocette (F444)

AC/Ford/Shelby Cobra (F381)
Austin-Healey 'Frogeye' Sprite (F343)
Corvette Stingray 1963-1967 (F432)
Ferrari 250GTO (F308)
Fiat X1/9 (F341)
Ford Cortina 1600E (F310)
Ford GT40 (F332)
Jaguar E-Type (F370)
Jaguar D-Type & XKSS (F371)
Jaguar Mk 2 Saloons (F307)
Jaguar SS90 & SS100 (F372)
Lancia Stratos (F340)
Lotus Elan (F330)
Lotus Seven (F385)
MGB (F305)
MG Midget & Austin-Healey Sprite (except 'Frogeye') (F344)

Morris Minor Series MM (F412)
Morris Minor & 1000 (ohv) (F331)
Porsche 911 Carrera (F311)
Rolls-Royce Corniche (F411)
Triumph Stag (F342)

B29 Superfortress (F339)
Boeing 707 (F356)
Harrier (F357)
Mosquito (F422)
Phantom II (F376)
P51 Mustang (F423)
Sea King (F377)
Super Etendard (F378)
Tiger Moth (F421)

Great Western Kings (F426)
Intercity 125 (F428)
V2 'Green Arrow' Class (F427)

Further titles in this series will be published at regular intervals. For information on new titles please contact your bookseller or write to the publisher.

Super Profile

FOREWORD

I am especially pleased to have been given the opportunity of writing this Foulis Super Profile of the BSA A7 and A10. No one knows how many BSA A7 and A10 motorcycles were built. For almost 17 years these twin-cylinder models were in continuous production and throughout the 1950s they were one of the most popular and familiar sights on the road. A large proportion of BSA produce went to export and an A7 or A10 parallel twin must have been ridden in every corner of the World.

The Birmingham Small Arms Company were the world leaders in the mass manufacture of motorcycles. Their expertise was founded upon gun making in the mid-19th century, then the most advanced form of engineering. In peacetime the Company employed their machines and skilled workforce to make bicycles and eventually, motorcycles. For over 100 years the name BSA was a household word and products bearing the company's famous 'piled arms' trademark had a reputation for being sturdy, robust and dependable. The A7 and later A10 machines were typical of this long tradition.

The BSA twins covered a wide range of aspects, and were adaptable to many forms of motorcycling. Most models were essentially for family men, being well suited for hauling a sidecar, yet in solo form the powerful twin-cylinder engine supplied the sporting enthusiast with a machine capable of outstanding performance. I hope this book will give an insight into these prodigious motorcycles and re-kindle happy memories for former owners of Star Twins, Shooting Stars, Golden Flashes, Road Rockets, Super Rockets and that diamond of all British motorcycles, the Rocket Gold Star. I'm sure that the following pages will form a useful guide for owner-riders and provide something of interest for even the most ardent A7/A10 enthusiast.

Yet another book about BSA motorcycles has been produced with the kind assistance and help of Barry (Polly) Palmer, proprietor of Bri-Tie Motorcycles, Swindon, and president of the BSA Owners Club. I am grateful for being given the privilege of being able to 'tap' Polly's extensive store of BSA information. In addition, my thanks go to Dave Hurson and Alan Lightfoot for allowing me a long interrogation whilst supplying me with many hints and tips to pass on to other A7 and A10 owners.

I must also express my gratitude to the many riders within the BSA Owners Club who have unknowingly supplied all the small snips of information that came together in researching this book, in particular the East Midlands 'Hard Core' who run up thousands of miles in the Black Horse at Walcote. For supplying some very useful photos my thanks go to Mr. R G J Watson, Chairman of Watsonian Sidecars, Jeff Allen – Editor of 'The Star', Bill Burdett and Barry Smith of South California, USA. I an also grateful to Ken Nelson of Three Legged Cross, Dorset and Bert Smith of Easton, Nr Wells, Somerset, who so kindly made their respective machines available for photography.

Finally, the guiding assistance and advice given by Jeff Clew will, no doubt, ensure that the BSA A7 and A10 Twins will be another worthy addition to the Super Profile series.

Owen Wright

Super Profile

HISTORY

The BSA A7 twin originated from those fraught days just prior to World War 2. It was in a well advanced state of development at the outbreak of the conflict and it was intended to include the model in the 1940 catalogue. Instead, the Company had other overriding issues to contend with, namely the high volume manufacture of military hardware. The still-born A7 underwent further attention during the war, but only when time and materials allowed.

The A7 was designed and developed by a number of prominent motorcycle designers who each, in turn, spent a period of time on the project and added their own contribution to a concept that was to be in production for 17 years and influence further ohv parallel twin construction until the Company collapsed in 1973.

Valentine Page, a highly skilled engineer, designed what was probably the first practical ohv parallel twin-cylinder motorcycle for the Triumph Company in 1933, a '650', designated the model 6/1. The machine was expensive and very few were sold, but it set a precedent and provided a useful learning ground for consequent designs. The first of these was Edward Turner's Triumph Speed Twin of 1937.

The Speed Twin took the two-wheeler world by storm due to Turner's flair for drawing an aesthetically pleasing and compact design. The bike was a 500cc twin but looked no bigger than a single, and weighed little more. With graceful styling and finished in an all-over coat of Amaranth Red, it called the tune for the other manufacturers, including BSA, to follow.

All the post World War 2 twin-cylinder motorcycles broadly followed the Speed Twin line in having both pistons rising and falling together on a 360 degree crankshaft, but they all had one distinctive and important feature and this was in the method of driving a camshaft and the position it occupied in the engine. When Val Page had drawn up the Triumph 6/1, he used a single camshaft lying across the engine behind and just below the cylinders. It was most certainly Page who specified and adopted this important configuration for the BSA A7 when he came over to the Small Heath factory in 1937, primarily to re-design a full range of single cylinder models. His work had also outlined the future BSA telescopic forks and some prototype twin-cylinder engines, one of which became the A7, foundation of all the A group twins. From basic concept to the first production model, much of the overall detail work on the A7 had been the responsibility of Herbert Perkins, a well-respected and long-serving BSA design engineer. It was during the War that Edward Turner had a brief spell with BSA and left his mark on the A7 project, using some of the classic features that had appeared on his Triumph Speed Twin machine. His eye for shape and styling was put to great effect by profiling a three-lobed outer timing cover. Although it did undergo a significant alteration in geometry, it gave the BSA twin its own unmistakable and eye catching signature.

In September 1946 the first production A7 was announced to an awaiting public that had already been given some brief but tempting reviews by the motorcycle press. The A7 was a typical BSA product, not a super-sports model intended for the racing clubman (although some gave it a good try) but a dependable workhorse for everyday use. It was a machine that could be serviced in a backyard with just a few basic tools. It was a part of BSA's long-standing tradition to provide the faithful family transport. In the showroom, or parked on the pavement outside a main street BSA dealership, the new A7 was an exciting prospect for those hard-pressed times. It was a perfect balance between old and new fashions, poised ready to take on the Triumph and steal some of its shine.

Although the engine went through a major modification every four years, it never strayed from the general layout of the first production model. Here is a description of the early A7 engine:

At the heart of the engine was a pair of 62mm diameter pistons rising and falling together on an 82mm stroke, giving a total swept volume of 495cc. The flat-topped 6.5:1 compression pistons carried three rings, and were connected to H section steel-forged conrods by fully floating gudgeon pins, retained at each end with a wire circlip. At the bottom end a one-piece crankshaft forged out of nickel-steel had a flywheel bolted axially to the central web. The crank had plain journals, with the con-rod big-end connected by separate bolted-on caps to locate a pair of plain shell bearings. This enabled a worn crank to be reground and undersized shell bearings fitted.

Following normal British engine practice, the left-hand side of the power unit formed the drive or transmission side. At this end the crankshaft was supported on a ball bearing located in an aluminium alloy crankcase. On the right-hand side, a plain white-metal bush served not only as the opposite crank bearing but also worked as an oil distributor directing oil to the big-end bearings through drillings in the crankshaft. The bush received a flow of lubricant from a two-stage pump driven from the crank by a worm gear. Oil flung up by the crank assembly deposited itself onto the cylinder bores. The oil drained down to the bottom of the crankcases and collected into a small detachable sump where it was picked up by the scavenge side of the oil pump and returned to the tank. The pressure side of the oil feed had a relief valve accessible from the front of the engine. A bleed off from the pressure line gave a steady feed to the timing gear train.

In between the timing side bush and the worm, a small pinion drove an idler gear at half engine speed. This, in turn, spun a four-lobed camshaft that ran across the rear of the engine. The final element in this geartrain was a two-pole Lucas K2F magneto with its own automatic advance and retard unit.

The camshaft gear had a peg which located and drove a timed engine breather to relieve crankcase pressure. An inner timing cover was screwed to the crankcase half and enabled the idler and cam gears to be simply supported between bushes pressed into the case and cover. Outboard of the inner cover, the overhung end of the idler gear shaft had a taper to accept a $\frac{5}{16}$in. pitch simplex sprocket. This drove a dynamo lying across the front of the engine, just below the cylinder barrels.

The camshaft operated a set of pushrods through a system of tappets. On these early engines the tappets were housed in sleeves which were, in turn, located into the upper edge of the crankcase. From here, the pushrods extended upwards towards their respective valve rockers. The outer rods were shorter in length and were inclined at a more vertical angle.

The cylinder barrel was a one-piece casting with an integral pushrod tunnel cleverly cored out between the cylinders. It was bolted down to the crankcase with eight nuts seated on the flange which formed the base of the cylinder block casting. A cast iron cylinder head was fastened down to the barrels but separated with a copper-asbestos gasket. Nine bolts were equally spaced around and between the combustion chambers to ensure a sufficient seal. Each pair of valves shared a combined well and ran in cast-iron guides pressed into the cylinder head. They used double coil springs retained with split tapered collets and a top-hat collar. Inside the cylinder head casting the inlet tracts ran parallel into hemispherical combustion chambers. The exhaust ports splayed outwards to accept a pushed in exhaust pipe. Each of the two separate rocker boxes consisted of an alloy casing containing a long fixed spindle on which the rockers acted, the casing of which bolted to the head. Square headed valve adjuster screws were accessible through screwed-in hexagonal caps. This meant that owners had to follow a tip given by Triumph owners and use a feeler gauge bent at the end. Valve and rocker lubrication depended upon oil mist working its way up the pushrod tunnel. The rear face of the cylinder head was machined to accept a separate manifold and a $\frac{15}{16}$in. type 276 Amal carburettor complete with a drip shield to avoid any excess petrol falling onto the magneto lying below.

A four-speed foot change gearbox with positive stop mechanism was bolted to the rear of the crankcase. In being so it gave fixed centres between crankshaft and gearbox mainshaft. A duplex primary chain connected the shafts and was tensioned by means of an adjustable slipper. The outboard end of the crank carried a two-lobed shock absorber whilst the gearbox shaft was tapered and keyed to take a six-spring and five-friction plate clutch. The primary drive had a polished alloy cover screwed to an inner case to allow the chain to run in an oil bath. The clutch was designed to run dry and was fitted with a pressed steel cover.

The whole power unit sat in an entirely new frame. Basically this was a duplex cradle type with a rigid rear end and telescopic front forks. It consisted of tubes brazed into forged connecting lugs. One of the unusual features of the early A7 was a peculiar type of centre stand, lowered by a ratchet lever. The idea was impractical and downright dangerous if the ratchet mechanism failed. It was quietly dispensed with and probably became the first casualty in a long history of modifications and developments applied to the twins.

A fuel tank and sprung saddle bolted to frame lugs. The fuel tank housed a speedometer, in pre-war fashion. Another short lived item on the A7 concerned the wheels, not so much the fact that they were quickly detachable but that they could be interchanged. Both brakes were of the half width hub type, of 7in. diameter and operated by cable at the front and by rod at the rear.

The A7 first appeared in an all-over Devon Red finish that tended to 'mirror' the Triumph Speed Twin colouring. The fuel tank was chromed with a gold lined red top and side panels. Similar treatment was given to the wheel rims, with the central band in red. A more sober black and chrome version was offered. The new BSA twin cost £171.

The early or 'longstroke' A7 as it became known fulfilled its promise by delivering 26 bhp at the back wheel with the engine running at 6000 rpm. Top speed was about 85 mph. The real strength of a BSA twin ever since these early models, and right up to the last, was its ability to keep up a steady cruising speed all day, without any flagging. The A7 could do this easily at a constant 60 mph, with a fuel consumption of the order of 65-70 mpg. It did have a few teething problems, the most noticeable being an awkward gearshift operation in the gearbox. As for the engine, sticking exhaust valves due to a build up of carbon could be an irritation. Some riders complained (albeit in a light hearted vein) that the engine would 'run on', long after the magneto cut-out button had been pressed, though the low octane fuel, then described as 'pool' petrol, took most of the blame.

Compared to its Triumph arch rival, the BSA was a lot quieter, with no valve gear rattle. It was always the more durable and longer lasting between rebores and crank regrinds. It has to be admitted, though, that the Triumph always had that extra 'zest' and the will to pull faster. The general pattern was set right from these early days and would carry on as both makes were continually up-rated and ran neck and neck in the race to win custom.

In an act of sheer boldness, the A10 was given some very flamboyant styling and a colour that would set it apart from anything else seen on the roads. BSA applied an all-over coat of golden-beige. Compared to most other vehicles on the roads at that time, the A10 presented a majestic sight. To compliment its colour, the A10 was given a name that ultimately became a household word; they called it the Golden Flash. Only a mighty 1000cc V-twin Vincent could outpoint a Golden Flash for speed, reliability, economy and the ability to cruise all day with or without a sidecar attached.

The A10 had instant appeal and attraction. It soon became a favourite with sidecar users, police forces and soloists intent on serious touring. BSA had shown faith in their own products, for when the production drawings were still being finalised, the go-ahead was given to prepare jigs, fixtures and all the necessary tooling before any serious testing had been carried out. Bert Hopwood's design team gritted their teeth and waited as three prototype A10s were given a rigorous and continuous run with an array of test riders taking turns and running up 4,000 miles a week for each bike. No major problems were reported.

The A10 Golden Flash was the star of the October 1949 Show and the first models were available by early November. It offered 35 bhp at 5500 rpm. Top speed was about 95 mph, though braver riders with a well set-up engine and a supporting wind could just about reach beyond that tempting 100 mph mark. Fuel consumption was in the order of 65 mpg for a solo cruising at a steady 60-70 mph, whilst sidecar users could see a return of 50-55 mpg at a similar speed. The Golden Flash was given a price tag of £193 with a rigid frame and £205 for the spring frame.

Only a few blemishes marked an otherwise exciting and sturdy machine. The problem of carbon build up on the exhaust valve stem still persisted. Plunger-framed machines were a whole lot more comfortable on a long run but handling wasn't quite as good on rough and twisty roads, due to the plungers allowing too much rear wheel side movement. A heavy sidecar could ruin the rear QD hub spline and take a fair toll of wheel bearings.

After just a few months of A10 production, Bert Hopwood applied his modifications to the A7 and A7 Star Twin. By the middle of 1951 production of the 500s in their near-original form ceased. The new A7 was bored out to 66mm and its stroke shortened to 72.6mm, to give a slightly raised engine capacity of 497cc. Both A7 & A10 shared 95% of components. It had always been Bert Hopwood's belief that it made economical sense to have different capacity machines built on a modular basis. A little later, he had a prototype 250cc ohv single built. It was based upon the new type A7 and even used some of the 500 twin's parts. We can only wonder what difference it would have made to BSA's long-term fortunes.

One of the most amazing events ever to occur in the annals of motorcycling took place in 1952. BSA decided to try and win the coveted Maudes Trophy and asked the ACU to select, at random, three A7 Star Twins from the production line. The machines were taken on a long arduous tour of Europe where they also competed in the International Six Days Trial. All the riders were BSA personnel, these being; Fred Rist, Brian Martin, and Norman Vanhouse. Each rider carried away a gold medal and together they walked off with the team vase. Another journey through Northern Europe and Scandinavia was taken, including a timed sprint at Oslo. The machines were closely observed throughout and no problems were ever experienced after 4,500 demanding miles. It was an incredible achievement.

1953 saw the arrival of the first sports version of the A10. This was the export only A10 Super Flash. It had a higher lift camshaft, an Amal TT carburettor and an increase in compression ratio to 8:1 as against 6.5:1 for the Golden Flash. The motor gave a 42 bhp output and was housed in a plunger frame. It also boasted a rev counter and shallow valanced mudguards. It was a pity that very few of these machines found their way onto the home market.

The following year saw another sporting success, once more attributed to the A7 Star Twin. The occasion was the 200 mile 'experts' race at Daytona beach, USA. Though the race was 'designed' for the Harley-Davidson V-Twins, two A7 Star Twins came home in 1st and 2nd positions, causing some very long faces amongst the home crowd. This wasn't helped at all when the following three places were taken by BSA Gold Star singles!

At home, 1954 saw the introduction of the swinging arm frame and the phasing out of the old plunger models. The new frame was of all-welded construction. The rear wheel fork was pivoted on a

Super Profile

set of rubber-bonded Silentbloc bushes at the base of the frame. Up and down movement of the fork was controlled by a pair of Girling shock-absorbers. The gearbox was separated from the engine and supported in plates bolted to the frame. This type of pre-unit construction was then the most common form of design practice. It meant that a Simplex $\frac{1}{2}$ in. pitch primary chain could be adjusted by pulling the gearbox back with an adjustable drawbolt. More importantly, BSA could now use their heavy duty gearbox and a whole range of wide and narrow ratio gear clusters. Handling was improved to exemplary standards.

The plunger framed 'specials', namely the A7 Star Twin and the A10 Super Flash, were dropped from the catalogue, to be replaced with swinging arm versions carrying new names, the A7 Shooting Star and the A10 Road Rocket. These two models had an alloy cylinder head. This allowed more efficient heat dispersal, enabling higher compression ratios to be used as well as achieving the obvious reduction in weight. The standard A7 and A10 Golden Flash continued with cast-iron heads.

Overall, the swinging arm twins had a more sleek appearance. Colour schemes continued much as before, with the A10 Golden Flash still available in all-over golden-beige, and the A7 in maroon, with black options for all models. The Road Rocket was for export only, leaving the A7 Shooting Star to be the obtainable home market special.

There were no changes to the engine internals but new crankcases had to be cast for the revised gearbox arrangement. It was impossible to exchange engines between swinging arm and plunger framed machines. The removal of the old type models from the showrooms caused an outcry. The ever-conservative sidecar people wouldn't accept the new frame – they claimed it lurched to and fro compared to their trusty old plunger versions. BSA relented and kept the plunger A10 Golden Flash in production for four more years.

At long last the A10 Road Rocket became available from local dealers in 1956. It was an immediate sensation in the hands of 'by-pass' sportsmen. It pushed out 40 bhp at 6000 rpm and a top speed of 109 mph could be attained. Acceleration was equally impressive, 0 to 60 mph in just under 8 seconds. The Road Rocket came fully equipped with matching speedometer and rev counter, a type TT9 carburettor and manual ignition advance-retard control. A red fuel tank and chromed mudguards were its hallmark.

During 1958 the Road Rocket was uprated further by modifying the alloy cylinder head and re-named the A10 Super Rocket. It could cruise comfortably for long periods at speeds in excess of 75 mph, matched by precise handling and firm suspension.

Since that sensational victory at Daytona, the BSA twins hardly ever appeared in the sporting news, except in minor grass-track events, where the low speed and high torque characteristics of the engine proved to be a boon for clubmen racing on the cheap. However, there were some other notable achievements.

In 1951, an attempt was made by the American dealership to breach the one mile records at Bonneville salt flats, when Gene Thiessen achieved 123.69 mph on a mildly improved production A7 Star Twin. For the unrestricted class, a highly modified A10 Golden Flash running on a Methanol/Benzole brew took the flying mile record at 143.54 mph. But, Triumph had already stolen a march on BSA with their own record breaking efforts on the same speed strip, and used the Bonneville name for their top of the range models.

The only time a BSA won an International Tourist Trophy on the Isle of Man was when Chris Vincent, piloted his famous A7 Shooting Star-engined 'kneeler' outfit. With Eric Bliss in the chair this unexpected but popular win in 1962 was achieved at an average speed of 83.57 mph.

There was one particular event that has never received much of a mention, but, for my money it typified what the twin was all about. Early in 1960, Bob Forrest-Webb, the founding Editor of *Motorcycle Mechanics* arranged for two A10 Golden Flash/Watsonian combo's to make a 4500 mile trek from London to the southern rim of the Sahara desert and back again. He took with him racer and tuner Geoff Monty, who rode one of the outfits. Acting as official photographer on the journey was Ron Spillman. He occupied a seat in Forrest-Webb's outfit and was able to record the appalling conditions experienced on the way, which varied from ice-bound 'pavé' roads through France to the rock-strewn dust tracks of the sweltering desert. The trek took just two weeks. No major breakdowns were experienced, thanks to Geoff Monty's mechanical know-how.

Having bought the Ariel Motor Company during the war, BSA arranged for the Selly Oak factory to build an up-market A10. It was called the Ariel Huntmaster and employed a number of cosmetic alterations to distinguish it from the stock BSA. The Huntmaster was a well respected machine. It appeared in 1954 with a swinging arm frame and remained in production for four years.

After the export only Super Flash, there were a number of special models made for the American market. Amongst these were the Royal Tourist and the A10 Spitfire Scrambler, the latter of which influenced the home market models in that the Spitfire camshaft was fitted to the late swinging arm models.

Another spin-off from the BSA twin concerned a machine that was a rarity in this country but very popular in far eastern Asia, the Japanese Meguru K-1. It was strongly based upon the A7, even using the same 66 x 72.6 mm bore and stroke. The argument still persists as to whether BSA officially sold the manufacturing rights. However, we do know that the Japanese recognised the potential of the A7 and developed it further. When Kawasaki absorbed the Meguro factory they carried on making a bored out version that boasted 53 bhp, a top speed of 105 mph and a whole range of improvements such as disc brakes and a 90 watt dynamo. The final W-3 model was in production until 1976!

Times were changing fast in the early 60s. The days of the faithful family Golden Flash were passing as more and more small and cheap saloon cars became available to the masses. The sidecarists were defecting to four wheels in droves as the BSA twin became more of an outright sports machine, constantly developed to meet ever increasing demands for pure power and speed. By 1962, BSA had introduced some completely new 500 and 650cc twins, with engine and gearbox combined in unit construction – the A50 and A65. These machines were cheaper to build, easier to maintain and on paper should have been the natural successors to the A7 and A10 models. BSA enthusiasts were sceptical about the change but were informed by BSA publicity that the move was prompted by the fact that Lucas would not make any more magnetos or dynamos.

When production of the A7 and A7 Shooting Star ceased in 1962, the A10 models were given another lease of life when the company was persuaded by Gold Star specialist Eddie Dow to make one final version, the A10 Rocket Gold Star. It was built by selecting the best Super Rocket engines from the test bench and fitting them into a Gold Star frame. A truly incredible motorcycle embodying all the finest BSA engineering. It was capable of reaching beyond 115 mph from an engine rated at 46 bhp at 6250 rpm. About 1500 Rocket Gold Stars were produced. Many optional extras were available such as a 'Lyta' 5 gallon fuel tank, siamese exhaust system and alloy fork yokes, to name just a few. By the middle of 1963 the A50 and A65 were becoming somewhat begrudgingly accepted and as sports versions of these bikes were being considered, the last few A10 variants were being crated up and despatched finally and for all time.

It would take a very educated guess to estimate the total number of machines produced. All we know is that BSA had provided the motorcycling world with one of the most popular machines ever built. It was a motorcycle that had endeared itself to the public and won the admiration and respect of even the most ardent enthusiast. The sight of a BSA twin during its heyday in the 1950s conjured a feeling of stability and invincibility, not just for BSA, but for the whole of the British motorcycle industry.

Super Profile

EVOLUTION

It wasn't too long before BSA followed their normal policy by bringing out up-rated versions of a standard model. At the Autumn 1949 Earls Court Show, a new model called the A7 'Special' was unveiled. The engine had a twin-carburettor set up and a higher compression ratio. More noticeable to the show visitors though was a frame with plunger rear springing. The tank and wheel rims were painted in matt silver, with the frame and front forks in black. The tank carried a large silver star to further distinguish it from the ordinary version. By the time it went into production, it had been re-named the A7 Star Twin. Modifications increased its power output to 31 bhp at 6000 rpm.

The Star Twin received much acclaim in contemporary test reports, although it was hardly any faster than the standard A7. Those fortunate enough to have tried both models would say that the second carburettor made little difference.

Earlier in 1948 the Company produced a special one-off trials A7 for works rider Bill Nicholson. Although Nicholson reverted to using a Gold Star single after just one season with the A7, it did show that the ohv Twin was versatile and strong enough for traversing rough terrain.

Whilst both A7 models continued in production, with just a few cosmetic changes, some events back at the BSA Small Heath factory brought about the most significant change in the model's history — the birth of the 650cc A10.

There were a number of reasons why BSA wanted a '650' twin in the catalogue. A high percentage of machines were despatched overseas and the American market in particular wanted something larger than a 500 to compare more favourably with their own large capacity V-twins, whilst at home a 650 would be a more attractive proposition for pulling a sidecar. Also, it was no secret that Triumph were planning to introduce their new 650cc Thunderbird model.

A bored out A7 was tried at first, but its performance didn't come up to expectations. The A7 still had a few niggling problems for the engineers to sort out. The gearbox footchange trouble was regarded as serious and this prompted the management to call in Bert Hopwood.

Hopwood had been working in a secluded office at Small Heath as a 'Forward Product Engineer' delving into the feasibility of future designs. He cured the gearbox fault in just a few hours, only to find that his brief had been extended to drawing up a 650 twin to be known as the A10.

They say it took Bert Hopwood just 10 days to draw the design schemes for the A10. It may only have been a re-vamped A7 in concept, but the number of modifications specified were many.

The A10 had a 70mm by 84mm bore and stroke, giving a capacity of 646cc. The separate rocker boxes used on the A7 were replaced with a one-piece alloy casing, with oblong inspection covers that gave access to either pair of valves. The cylinder head was also completely revised by having an induction manifold 'cast-in' to take a single carburettor. The exhaust valves sat in separate wells to allow a more effective flow of cooling air.

Inside the engine, the con-rod material was changed from steel to alloy and the pistons were of the split-skirt type, chosen to control expansion and allow closer running tolerances for an even quieter engine. The drive side ball bearing was changed to a roller type. Underneath the camshaft, a gully was cast into the cases so that the cams ran in an oil bath.

At a first glance the A7 and A10 looked the same. Both models used a similar frame, either rigid or plunger. But the new A10 used an improved 60 watt dynamo in place of the earlier 40 watt unit. Its position was raised slightly and this meant that the outer timing side cover had a more symmetrical look, giving the power unit a compact impression.

Production changes

The first BSA ohv parallel twin was launched in September 1946 and designated the model A7, having an engine capacity of 495cc (62 x 82mm) built in semi-unit construction with the gearbox. The specification included magneto ignition, 40 watt dynamo/battery lighting, rigid frame with telescopic front forks, 7 in brakes, front and rear. Frames and engines were stamped from XA7 — 101. The All-over finish was in Devon Red with winged B motif on tank.

1947: From engine number XA7-601, the big-end journal was reduced in diameter from 1.47 in to 1.46 in. From engine number XA7-450, an oil feed to the exhaust rocker gear was added. A black and chrome finish was now standard, with Devon Red as an option. Higher compression pistons were available.

In October, the A10 Golden Flash was shown for the first time, with an engine capacity of 646cc

(70 x 84mm). It had a one-piece rocker box, and tappets located in the cylinder block. The number of cylinder flange nuts was increased from 8 to 9. The drive side main bearing was of the radial ball type, otherwise the engine was similar to that of the A7. The frame was also similar to that of the A7, with both rigid and plunger options. There was an 8in brake at the front, and a 60 watt Lucas E3L dynamo was fitted. The machine finish was all-over Golden Beige with chrome, and there was a black and chrome option. The petrol tank had a circular 'Golden Flash' badge. The first engine and frame was stamped ZA10-101.

1948: From engine number YA7-3403, an oil feed was given to both inlet and exhaust rockers.

1949: After frame number ZA7-101, the wheels were no longer interchangeable. A revised rear wheel QD arrangement was adopted, using a splined hub.

The A7 Star Twin was introduced. It had twin carburettors and a plunger frame, and a silver on chrome tank finish, with a star-type badge. A plunger frame was optional for the standard A7.

1950: From engine numbers ZA10-1215 and ZA7 – 11192 the gearbox feaured a modified layshaft and a new gear cluster.

1951: The A7 and A7 Star Twin had a new engine incorporating features applied to A10. The new engine capacity was 497cc (66 x 72.6mm). The A7 Star Twin now had one carburettor only. The last 'longstroke' A7 was stamped ZA7-11192. The new type A7s started from AA7-101. The A10 from engine number ZA10-4712 and the new A7 models had lubrication drillings in the camshaft gulley and one hole in the left-hand con-rod. (Con-rods no longer interchangeable).

1952: Production of the rigid frames ceased. Due to shortages of chromium, the fuel tanks were painted all over. A new type headlamp unit with pre-focus bulb and underslung pilot light was fitted. Dual seats were now available. The A7 Star Twin had a manual ignition control.

1953: A revised rear light/number plate unit was introduced, which blended in with the mudguard. The headlamp now had a pressed steel cowl/fork shroud. An 8in front brake was given to the A7 models. The fork oil capacity was increased from $\frac{1}{4}$ to $\frac{3}{8}$ pint for all models. The A7 had chrome stripping on the petrol tank (this year only). Introduced for export only was the A10 Super Flash, with an 8:1 compression ratio, rev counter and other extras.

1954: The swinging arm frame was introduced with rear damping controlled by Girling shock absorbers. A new style $5\frac{1}{2}$ pint oil tank and matching tool box were fitted to the frame. The petrol tank was now retained by a single bolt. A separate BSA heavy series gearbox was used, with revised gear ratios. The primary chain was now of the $\frac{1}{2}$in pitch Simplex type, adjusted by a drawbolt. Only the A10 Golden Flash was retained in plunger frame form.

A new A7 Shooting Star replaced the A7 Star Twin and A10 Road Rocket replaced the 'export only' Super Flash. Both models had alloy cylinder heads. The A7 Shooting Star was available in a dark green frame, with polychromatic green tanks, toolbox and mudguards. A circular 'Gold Star' type tank badge was fitted. The A10 RR had a red tank with a round 'piled arms' type tank badge and chrome mudguards. Black and chrome options were available for all models.

1955: A new headlamp was fitted, with integral pilot lamp. An Amal Monobloc carburettor was now standard equipment, except on the A10 Road Rocket. New, slimmer suspension units were fitted and mudguards were made from a single pressing. Later in the year, Ariel-type alloy full width hubs were employed (except on the plunger A10). Brakes were 7in diameter, front and rear. The rear brake was controlled via cross-over shaft running in the hollow swing arm pivot shaft. The final linkage between the cross-over shaft and the rear hub was by cable. The A7 was available in all-over maroon.

1956: A 4-piece pressed steel fully enclosed chainguard became optional equipment for all models. The alloy cylinder heads now had integral inlet ports for a direct bolting carburettor.

1957: No changes. This was the last year of manufacture of the plunger-type A10 Golden Flash.

1958: Re-styled cycle parts. The oil tank and tool box had a rounded outer surface. The headlamp, ammeter and lighting switch were housed in a nacelle/fork shroud. The full width hubs were changed to the Triumph cast-iron type, with straight pull spokes. The front brake had a slotted boss instead of a torque arm. Oval-shaped silencers were fitted. For the A10 Golden Flash only there was a revised engine with its cylinder base flange thickness increased from $\frac{3}{8}$in to $\frac{1}{2}$in. The big-end journals were increased in diameter to 1.687in. The crankshaft was now made in EN16B steel, and the flywheel retained by 3 radial bolts. There was also an enlarged sludge trap area. The new A10 engine was stamped DA10-. All frames were painted black, but the tanks, toolboxes and mudguards remained in their previous optional colours.

A 'piled arms' transfer was applied to the oil tank and the tool box worded 'BSA Motor Cycles Ltd', ' (previously 'BSA Cycles Ltd').

The performance of the A10 Road Rocket was increased and the model re-named the A10 Super Rocket. The frames had a revised roll-on centre stand, and the sidecar lugs were repositioned.

Super Profile

1959: All models were fitted with sports type camshafts, as used on the A7SS and A10SR models. Pear-shaped tank badges and small knee grips were given to some A7, A10GF and A10SR models. The A10SR model was available in a silver grey and the A7 in Princess Grey.

The A10 Spitfire Scrambler was introduced for export only. It had many special fittings and extras. The engine was basically of the Super Rocket type.

1960: From engines numbers CA7-8624, CA7SS-8113 and DA10-13299, a Triumph four spring clutch was fitted as standard. This unit was supported on 20 rollers running on the mainshaft sleeve. The previous BSA six-spring version had used a double row ball bearing. A drain plug incorporating an oil level standpipe was provided in the chaincase cover. An adjustment access plug was provided in the chaincase cover. An Amal TT9 carburettor became an optional extra for A10SR model. All models were fitted with revised and slimmer valanced mudguards. A Wipac 3-position dip switch was fitted to the handlebar on the left-hand side. A rev counter was another optional extra (standard fitting for the A10SR). The drive was taken from the oil pump instead of the magneto drive pinion, as previously.

Pear-shaped badges were now used on all models, except some A7SS. The A10 Golden Flash was available in Sapphire Blue. A DA10 series engine was now fitted to the Super Rocket model.

1961: Some A10 Golden Flash models were fitted with a crankshaft-mounted alternator (intended for police forces and the export market).

1962: From February, the A10 Rocket Gold Star was introduced. It was based on the Super Rocket engine fitted to a Gold Star frame, with a wide range of options and extras which included a close-ratio gearbox, Gold Star 190mm front brake, Lyta 5 gall fuel tank and a siamese exhaust system with a Gold Star silencer. The A7 and A7SS models were discontinued.

1963: In July, all the pre-unit twins were discontinued.

SPECIFICATION

Early A7 models				
Model	A7		A7 Star Twin	
Year of manufacture	1946/50		1949/50	
Capacity (cc)	495		495	
Bore & stroke (mm)	62 x 82		62 x 82	
Compression ratio	6.6:1[1]		7.0:1[2]	
Bhp	26 @ 6000 rpm		31 @ 6000 rpm	
Gear ratios	Solo	Sidecar	Solo	Sidecar
4th	5.11	5.44	5.11	5.44
3rd	6.19	6.93	6.19	6.93
2nd	8.99	9.57	8.99	9.57
1st	13.19	14.05	13.19	14.05
Sprocket sizes				
Engine	27		27	
Clutch	54		54	
Gearbox	18		18	
Rear wheel	46[3]		46[3]	

Super Profile

Chain sizes		
Primary	3/8 in Duplex x 80 pitches	3/8 in Duplex x 80 pitches
Rear	5/8 in x 3/8 in[4] x 102 pitches	5/8 in x 3/8 in[4] x 102 pitches
Suspension		
Front	telescopic	telescopic
Rear	rigid[5]	plunger
Tyre sizes		
Front	3.25 x 19in	3.25 x 19in
Rear	3.50 x 19in	3.50 x 19in
Brake drum		
Diameter and width		
Front	7in x 1 1/8 in	7in x 1 1/8 in
Rear	7in x 1 1/8 in	7in x 1 1/8 in
Fuel tank capacity	3.5 gall (Imp)[6]	3.5 gal (Imp)
Oil tank capacity	4 pints (Imp)	4 pints (Imp)
Gearbox capacity	1 pint (Imp)	1 pint (Imp)
Generator		
Type and output	Lucas E3H dynamo 40 watts	Lucas E3H dynamo 40 watts
Voltage & earth polarity	6 volt negative	6 volt negative
Ignition system	Lucas K2F Magneto	Lucas K2F Magneto
Points gap	0.010/0.012in	0.010/0.012in
Timing (BTDC)	3/8 in	3/8 in
Valve clearances	Inlet 0.015in / Exhaust 0.015in[7]	Inlet 0.015in / Exhaust 0.015in
Wheelbase (in)	54.5	55
Ground clearance (in)	6.5	5
Seat height (in)	29.5	31
O/A width (in)	29	29
Dry weight (lb)	365	382

Notes
1. 7.0:1 1946/47
2. 7.5:1 and 8.6:1 options
3. 49 teeth for sidecar
4. 103 pitches for sidecar
5. Plunger option 1949/50
6. 3 gall 1946
7. Up to engine XA7-601, 0.003in inlet and exhaust
8. 8in x 1 3/8 in from 1953

Super Profile

Model	A7		A7 Star Twin
Year of manufacture	1950/54		1950/54
Capacity (cc)	497		497
Bore & stroke (mm)	66 x 72.6		66 x 72.6
Compression ratio	6.6:1		7.25:1
Bhp	27 @ 5800 rpm		31 @ 6000 rpm
Gear ratios	Solo	Sidecar	Solo
4th	5.11	5.44	5.00
3rd	6.19	6.93	6.05
2nd	8.99	9.57	8.80
1st	13.19	14.05	12.90
Sprocket sizes			
Engine	27		27
Clutch	54		54
Gearbox	18		18
Rear wheel	46 (3)		46
Chain sizes			
Primary	$\frac{3}{8}$in Duplex x 80 pitches		$\frac{3}{8}$in Duplex x 80 pitches
Rear	$\frac{5}{8}$in x $\frac{3}{8}$in[4] x 102 pitches		$\frac{5}{8}$in x $\frac{3}{8}$in x 102 pitches
Suspension			
Front	telescopic		telescopic
Rear	rigid or plunger		plunger
Tyre sizes			
Front	3.25 x 19in		3.25 x 19in
Rear	3.50 x 19in		3.50 x 19in
Brake drum Diameter and width			
Front	7in x $1\frac{1}{8}$in		7in x $1\frac{1}{8}$in[8]
Rear	7in x $1\frac{1}{8}$in		7in x $1\frac{1}{8}$in
Fuel tank capacity	3.5 gall (Imp)[6]		3.5 gall (Imp)
Oil tank capacity	4 pints (Imp)		4 pints (Imp)
Gearbox capacity	1 pint (Imp)		1 pint (Imp)
Generator Type and output Voltage & earth polarity	Lucas E3L dynamo 60 watts 6 volt positive		Lucas E3L dynamo 60 watts 6 volt negative
Ignition system	Lucas K2F Magneto		Lucas K2F Magneto
Points gap	0.10/0.012in		0.010/0.012in
Timing (BTDC)	$\frac{5}{16}$in		$\frac{3}{8}$in

15

Valve clearances	Inlet 0.010in	Exhaust 0.016in[7]	Inlet 0.010in	Exhaust 0.016in
Wheelbase (in)	55		55	
Ground clearance (in)	4.5		4.5	
Seat height (in)	30		30	
O/A width (in)	29		29	
Dry weight (lb)	400		382	

Notes
1. 7.0:1 1946/47
2. 7.5:1 and 8.6:1 options
3. 49 teeth for sidecar
4. 103 pitches for sidecar
5. Plunger option 1949/50
6. 3 gall 1946
7. Up to engine XA7-601, 0.003in inlet and exhaust
8. 8in x 1$\frac{3}{8}$in from 1953

Later A7 models

Model	A7	A7 Shooting Star
Year of manufacture	1954/62	1954/62
Capacity (cc)	497	497
Bore & stroke (mm)	66 x 72.6	66 x 72.6
Compression ratio	6.6:1[9]	7.25:1[10]
Bhp	28 @ 5800 rpm	32 @ 6250 rpm
Gear ratios		
4th	5.28	5.28
3rd	6.39	6.39
2nd	9.29	9.29
1st	13.63	13.63
Sprocket sizes		
Engine	18	18
Clutch	43	43
Gearbox	19[11]	19[11]
Rear wheel	42	42
Chain sizes		
Primary	$\frac{1}{2}$in x 0.305in x 68 pitches	$\frac{2}{3}$in x 0.305in x 68 pitches
Rear	$\frac{5}{8}$in x $\frac{3}{8}$in x 98 pitches	$\frac{5}{8}$in x $\frac{3}{8}$in x 98 pitches

Suspension				
Front	telescopic		telescopic	
Rear	swinging arm		swinging arm	
Tyre sizes				
Front	3.25 x 19in		3.25 x 19in	
Rear	3.50 x 19in		3.50 x 19in	
Brake drum				
Diameter and width				
Front	7in x $1\frac{1}{8}$in[12]		8in x $1\frac{3}{8}$in[13]	
Rear	7in x $1\frac{1}{8}$in		7in x $1\frac{1}{8}$in	
Fuel tank capacity	4 gall (Imp)		4 gall (Imp)	
Oil tank capacity	5.5 pints (Imp)		5.5 pints (Imp)	
Gearbox capacity	0.7 pint (Imp)		0.7 pint (Imp)	
Generator				
Type and output	Lucas E3L dynamo		Lucas E3L dynamo	
	60 watts		60 watts	
Voltage & earth polarity	6 volt positive		6 volt positive	
Ignition system	Lucas K2F Magneto		Lucas K2F Magneto	
Points gap	0.010/0.012in		0.010/0.012in	
Timing (BTDC)	$\frac{5}{16}$in		$\frac{3}{8}$in	
Valve clearances	Inlet	Exhaust[14]	Inlet	Exhaust[15]
	0.010in	0.016in	0.008in	0.012in
Wheelbase (in)	56		56	
Ground clearance (in)	6		6	
Seat height (in)	30		30	
O/A width (in)	28		28	
Dry weight (lb)	425		416	

Notes
9. 7.25:1 after 1959
10. 8:1 after 1957
11. 17 teeth for sidecar
12. 8in x $1\frac{3}{8}$in for 1954/55 models
13. 7in x $1\frac{1}{8}$in for 1956/57 models
14. 0.008in inlet, 0.008in exhaust from 1958
15. 0.008 in inlet, 0.010in exhaust from 1958

Super Profile

Early A10 models

Model	A10 Golden Flash		A10 Super Flash	A10 Road Rocket
Year of manufacture	1950/54[16]		1953/54	1955/57
Capacity (cc)	646		646	646
Bore & stroke (mm)	70 x 84		70 x 84	70 x 84
Compression ratio	6.5:1		8.0:1	8.0:1
Bhp	35 @ 5500 rpm		41	40 @ 6000 rpm
Gear ratios	Solo	Sidecar		
4th	4.42	5.16	4.42	4.52
3rd	5.35	6.24	5.35	5.48
2nd	7.77	9.07	7.77	7.96
1st	11.41	13.31	11.41	11.68
Sprocket sizes				
Engine	27		27	21
Clutch	54		54	43
Gearbox	19		19	19
Rear wheel	42[17]		42[17]	42
Chain sizes				
Primary	$\frac{3}{8}$in Duplex x 80 pitches		$\frac{3}{8}$in Duplex x 80 pitches	$\frac{1}{2}$in x 0.305in x 69 pitches
Rear	$\frac{5}{8}$in x $\frac{3}{8}$in x 102 pitches[15]		$\frac{5}{8}$in x $\frac{3}{8}$in x 102 pitches[18]	$\frac{5}{8}$ x $\frac{3}{8}$in x 97 pitches
Suspension				
Front	telescopic		telescopic	telescopic
Rear	rigid or plunger		plunger	swinging arm
Tyre sizes				
Front	3.25 x 19in		3.25 x 19in	3.25 x 19in
Rear	3.50 x 19in		3.50 x 19in	3.50 x 19in
Brake drum Diameter and width				
Front	8in x $1\frac{3}{8}$in		8in x $1\frac{3}{8}$in	7in x $1\frac{1}{2}$in
Rear	7in x $1\frac{1}{8}$in		7in x $1\frac{1}{8}$in	7in x $1\frac{1}{2}$in
Fuel tank capacity (4)	4.25 gall (Imp)[19]		4.25 gall (Imp)	4 gall (Imp)
Oil tank capacity	4 pints (Imp)		4 pints (Imp)	5.5 pint (Imp)
Gearbox capacity	1 pint (Imp)		1 pint (Imp)	0.7 pint (Imp)
Generator Type and output Voltage & earth polarity	Lucas E3L dynamo 60 watts 6 volt positive		Lucas E3L dynamo 60 watts 6 volt positive	Lucas E3L dynamo 60 watts 6 volt positive
Ignition system	Lucas K2F Magneto		Lucas K2F Magneto	Lucas K2F Magneto

Points gap	0.010/0.012in	0.010/0.012in	0.010/0.012in
Timing (BTDC)	$\frac{11}{32}$	$\frac{3}{8}$in	$\frac{3}{8}$in
Valve clearances	Inlet Exhaust 0.010in 0.010in	Inlet Exhaust 0.008in 0.008in	Inlet Exhaust 0.008in 0.008in
Wheelbase (in)	55	55	56
Ground clearance (in)	4.5	4.5	6
Seat height (in)	30	30	30
O/A width (in)	28	28	$31\frac{3}{8}$
Dry weight (lb)	408	N/A	418

Notes
16. plunger A10 offered until 1958
17. 49 teeth for sidecar
18. 103 pitches for sidecar
19. 3.5 gall option 1950/51

Later A10 models

Model	A10 Golden Flash	A10 Super Rocket	A10 Rocket Gold Star
Year of manufacture	1954/63 (16)	1958/63	1962/63
Capacity (cc)	646	646	646
Bore & stroke (mm)	70 x 84	70 x 84	70 x 84
Compression ratio[16]	6.5:1[20]	8.3:1[21]	9.0:1
Bhp	34 @ 5750 rpm	42 @ 6000 rpm	46 @ 6250 rpm[22]
Gear ratios			
4th	4.52	4.52	4.52
3rd	5.48	5.48	5.48
2nd	7.96	9.97	6.00[23]
1st	11.68	11.68	7.93
Sprocket sizes			
Engine	21	21	23
Clutch	43	43	43
Gearbox	19	19	19
Rear wheel	42	42	46
Chain sizes			
Primary	$\frac{1}{2}$in x 0.305in x 69 pitches	$\frac{1}{2}$in x 0.305in x 69 pitches	$\frac{1}{2}$in x 0.305in x 70 pitches
Rear	$\frac{5}{8}$in x $\frac{3}{8}$in x 98 pitches	$\frac{5}{8}$in x $\frac{3}{8}$in x 98 pitches	$\frac{5}{8}$ x $\frac{3}{8}$in x 99 pitches
Suspension			
Front	telescopic	telescopic	telescopic (Gold Star type)
Rear	swinging arm	swinging arm	swinging arm

Super Profile

Tyre sizes			
Front	3.25 x 19in	3.25 x 19 in	3.25 x 19in
Rear	3.50 x 19in	3.50 x 19in	3.50 x 19in
Brake drum			
Diameter and width			
Front	8in x 1$\frac{3}{8}$in	8in x 1$\frac{3}{8}$in	8in x 1$\frac{3}{8}$in[24]
Rear	7in x 1$\frac{1}{8}$in	7in x 1$\frac{1}{8}$in	7in x 1$\frac{1}{8}$in
Fuel tank capacity	4 gall (Imp)	4 gal (Imp)	4 gall (Imp)[25]
Oil tank capacity	5.5 pints (Imp)	5.5 pints (Imp)	5.5 pints (Imp)
Gearbox capacity	0.7 pint (Imp)	0.7 pint (Imp)	0.7 pint (Imp)
Generator			
Type and output	Lucas E3L dynamo 60 watts	Lucas E3L dynamo 60 watts	Lucas E3L dynamo 60 watts
Voltage & earth polarity	6 volt positive	6 volt positive	6 volt positive
Ignition system	Lucas K2F magneto	Lucas K2F magneto	Lucas K2F magneto
Points gap	0.010/0.12in	0.010/0.012in	0.010/0.012in
Timing (BTDC)	$\frac{11}{32}$[26]	$\frac{3}{8}$in	$\frac{13}{32}$ in
Valve clearances	Inlet 0.010in / Exhaust 0.016in[27]	Inlet 0.08in / Exhaust 0.008in	Inlet 0.008in / Exhaust 0.010in
Wheelbase (in)	56	56	56
Ground clearance (in)	6	6	6
Seat height (in)	30	30	30
O/A width (in)	28	28	28
Dry weight (lb)	430	418	N/A

Notes
20. 7.25:1 from 1958
21. 9:1 for 1962/63
22. 50 bhp with Gold Star silencer
23. alternative ratio options
24. 190mm Gold Star options
25. 2 or 5 gall options
26. $\frac{13}{32}$in after engine DA10-1647
27. 0.008in inlet, 0.010in exhaust after engine DA10-1647

Carburettors

Model		Type	Choke size (in)	Main jet	Pilot jet	Throttle slide	Needle jet	Needle position
A7	1946-54	Amal 276	$\frac{15}{16}$	140	–	6/3[1]	.107	3
A7	1955-62	Amal 376 Monobloc	$\frac{15}{16}$	210	25	$3\frac{1}{2}$	.106	2
A7ST	1949-50	Amal 275 twin carb	$\frac{7}{8}$	110	–	5/4	.107	3
A7ST	1951-53	Amal 276 or Amal TT9	1 $1\frac{1}{16}$	160 350	– –	6/4 6	.107 .109	3 4
A7SS	1954	Amal 276	1	170	–	6/4	.107	3
A7SS	1955-62	Amal 376 Monobloc	1	270	30	$3\frac{1}{2}$	.106	3
A10GF	1950-54	Amal 276	$1\frac{1}{16}$	170	–	6/4	.108	2
A10GF	1955-59	Amal 376 Monobloc	$1\frac{1}{16}$	240	25	$3\frac{1}{2}$	.106	3
A10GF	1960-63	Amal 389 Monobloc	$1\frac{1}{8}$	250	30	$3\frac{1}{2}$	.106	3
A10RR	1954-57	Amal TT9	$1\frac{1}{16}$	340	–	6	.109	4
A10RR	1958	Amal 389 Monobloc	$1\frac{1}{8}$	290	30	$3\frac{1}{2}$	.106	3
A10SR	1958-59	Amal 376 Monobloc	$1\frac{1}{16}$	250	25	$3\frac{1}{2}$	.106	4
A10SR	1960-63	Amal 389 Monobloc or Amal TT9	$1\frac{5}{32}$ $1\frac{5}{32}$	420 410	25 –	3 7	.106 .109	2 4
A10RGS	1962-63	Amal 389 Monobloc	$1\frac{5}{32}$	310	25	3	.106	2

Notes
1. 1951-53, 6/4

Super Profile

ROAD TESTS

ROAD TESTS OF NEW MODELS

THE MOTOR CYCLE,

495 c.c. B.S.A. Model

Latest Edition of an Established High-performance Five-hundred

THE original 495 c.c. A7 B.S.A. was introduced to an eager, war-weary market in 1946 and retained its basic and detail design features almost without change until the end of last year. Though even to an experienced eye the 1951 engine and gear box exteriors are largely unchanged, both units are, in fact, new and almost identical in internal detail design with those of the already illustrious Golden Flash model. The result of the change-

The 1951 A7 is a cobby, neat, businesslike mount

over is such that many will immediately class the new A7 as being the best 500 c.c. B.S.A. yet; in terms of all-round engine performance, handling, braking and gear change—particularly the last—the new A7 is without doubt one of the best of two, or perhaps three, machines in its particular capacity class.

During the course of the Road Test, the B.S.A. was generally driven in a manner calculated to bring to light—and quickly—any indication that the engine might "fuss"

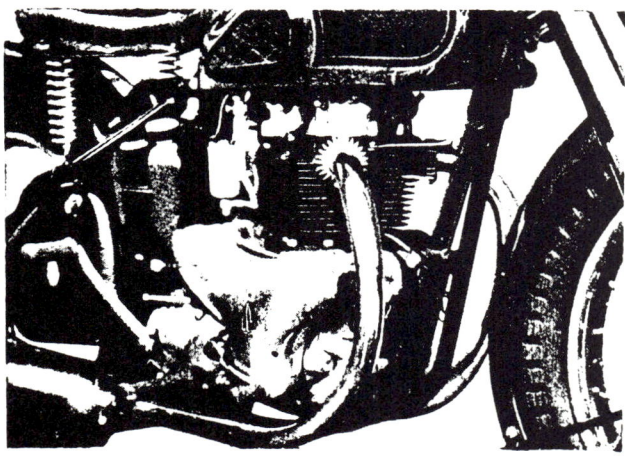

New twin-cylinder power unit follows closely the design of the 650 c.c. A10

or tire. In other words, the engine was revved very hard in the indirect ratios, and speeds wherever possible were just as high as road conditions permitted. On one particular occasion a run of 150 miles in Warwickshire and Shropshire was completed in a few minutes over three hours.

Speeds on the main roads were regularly in the 70-75 m.p.h. region, and 80 m.p.h. was maintained and held effortlessly on several occasions—this by a heavily garbed rider sitting in an orthodox position. When the machine was stopped after several miles on full bore, a hand could be placed on the cylinder finning. The exhaust pipes had not even discoloured near the ports; they later became slightly straw coloured, but never blue. Throughout the entire test the engine and gear box remained absolutely oil-tight. Transmission smoothness was of a high order. The rear chain, however, tended to run dry.

When motor cycling, there are naturally occasions when one begins a run with some fixed idea, such as: "I am going to potter," or, "I am out for a whang." Such were the A7's characteristics that, irrespective of the state of one's mind at the beginning of a run, speeds generally rose and rose throughout the run's duration. Reasons for this are not hard to seek; for instance, at 70 m.p.h. there is as complete lack of fuss as there is at 50-55 m.p.h. From 50 m.p.h. onwards, high-frequency vibration could be felt at the handlebar, but it was slight and would not worry even fastidious riders. Vibration was marked only when the engine was revved to the point of valve float.

A slow, reliable tick-over was one of the A7's most attractive features. At idling speeds, the engine was beautifully quiet mechanically, the only certainly identified noises being piston slap and slight "rustling" from the valve-gear. The built-in air cleaner completely eliminates induction hiss. Performance figures, incidentally, were taken with the filter in use. Pick-up throughout the entire throttle range was clean and brisk, and there was no undue tendency to pinking.

Slightly heavy in operation, the clutch freed perfectly at all times, required no adjustment even after the high stresses imposed when performance figures were being taken, and was delightfully smooth in its take-up. Bottom gear could be engaged noiselessly and certainly when the machine was stationary with the engine idling. Clean and entirely positive upward gear changes were accomplished by moving

8 February 1951

A7 Twin

Enthralling Machine

the pedal without due attention to making a deliberate lag in pedal movement. Snap racing-type changes could be made with certainty and with or without freeing the clutch. When snap changes were made, the pinions engaged with the merest suggestion of a "clonk." In the indirect ratios, notably in third gear, there was considerable gear whine. Clean, sweet, downward changes could be accomplished just as quickly as the controls could be operated. Pedal movement was short and light, and the pedal could be moved up or down by lightly pivoting the right foot on the footrest. The combination of positive gear change, clean pick-up and reliable idling made the B.S.A. particularly useful for safe, effortless traffic threading.

The front fork has a long, soft movement, allowing the front wheel to follow the road surface accurately, be it bumpy or smooth, be the speed high or low. Greasy cobbles and wet tramlines could be traversed with complete confidence. The rear suspension (which on the A7 is an extra) provided reasonable comfort, though slightly more travel, it was felt, would have been appreciated.

Light Brake Operation

Both brakes were smooth and progressive in operation, and provided adequate stopping power. Fade was never experienced under hard-driving conditions on the road, but it did occur when the braking figures were being taken —a quick succession of crash stops in this instance being made from 30 m.p.h. Both brakes were light in operation.

The only point of criticism applying to the riding position was that the top corners of the knee pads were slightly sharp and caused discomfort towards the end of a day in the saddle. Relationship between saddle, footrests and handlebar provided a comfortable knee angle and arm reach, and the angle of the grips allowed a natural position for the

Primary drive is by a duplex chain with a slipper for adjustment. Gear box is bolted to the rear of the crankcase

wrists. Both footrests and handlebar are, of course, adjustable. All controls were delightfully sweet in operation.

An intense and commendably wide driving beam was furnished by the 7in Lucas head lamp. In its position on the fork bridge, the speedometer was easily read by a normally seated rider. The instrument read approximately seven per cent fast. Mudguarding provided above-average protection for rider and machine. The centre stand could be operated without undue muscular effort, but required knack. The prop stand (which is an extra) was easily operated and held the machine safely.

Engine starting from cold (during some of the coldest weather experienced this winter) was certain at the third or fourth dig on the kick-starter. Kick-starting required commendably little physical effort or knack, and engendered the thought: "A child could do it." Finish of the A7 is black and chromium, with the tank finished in red and chromium.

B.S.A. 495 c.c. Model A7 twin

Information Panel

SPECIFICATION

ENGINE: 495 c.c. (66 x 72.6 mm) o.h.v. vertical twin. Fully enclosed valve gear operated by push rods from a single camshaft. Plain-bearing big-ends. Mainshaft supported by roller and plain bearings. Compression ratio, 6.7 to 1. Dry-sump lubrication; tank capacity, 4 pints.
CARBURETTOR: Amal; twistgrip throttle control; air-slide operated by handlebar lever. Built-in air cleaner.
IGNITION AND LIGHTING: Lucas magneto with auto-advance. Separate 45w Lucas dynamo. 7in. head lamp. 30/24w head lamp bulb.
TRANSMISSION: B.S.A. four-speed gear box with positive-stop foot control. Bottom, 13.2 to 1. Second, 9.0 to 1. Third, 6.2 to 1. Top, 5.1 to 1. Multi-plate clutch with fabric inserts. Primary chain, ⅜in duplex in cast-aluminium, light-alloy case. Secondary chain, ½ x ⅜in. R.p.m. at 30 m.p.h. in top gear, 1,990 approx.
FUEL CAPACITY: 3¼ gallons.
TYRES: Dunlop. Front 3.25 x 19in. Rear 3.50 x 19in. Both studded tread
BRAKES: 7 x 1⅛in front and rear.
SUSPENSION: B.S.A. telescopic front fork with hydraulic damping. Plunger-type rear springing.
WHEELBASE: 54¾in. Ground clearance, 4½in unladen.
SADDLE: Lycett. Unladen height, 30in
WEIGHT: 436lb with fuel and oil tanks full and machine fully equipped.
PRICE: £144 plus Purchase Tax (in Britain only), £38 17s 8d. Spring frame extra, £10, plus P.T. £2 14s.
ROAD TAX: £3 15s a year; £1 0s 8d a quarter.
MAKERS: B.S.A. Cycles, Ltd., Small Heath, Birmingham, 11.
DESCRIPTION: *The Motor Cycle*, 19 October, 1950

PERFORMANCE DATA

MEAN MAXIMUM SPEED: Bottom: 36 m.p.h.*
Second: 54 m.p.h.*
Third: 78 m.p.h.
Top: 88 m.p.h.
*Valve floating starting

MEAN ACCELERATION:

	10-30 m.p.h.	20-40 m.p.h.	30-50 m.p.h.
Bottom	2.4 secs	—	—
Second	4 secs	3 secs	3.2 secs.
Third	—	5.4 secs	5 secs
Top	—	8.2 secs	7.4 secs

Mean speed at end of quarter mile from rest: 76 m.p.h.
Mean time to cover standing quarter mile: 17.6 secs.
PETROL CONSUMPTION: At 30 m.p.h., 92 m.p.g. At 40 m.p.h. 81 m.p.g. At 50 m.p.h., 72 m.p.g. At 60 m.p.h., 64 m.p.g.
BRAKING: From 30 m.p.h. to rest, 29ft 6in (surface, wet tar macadam)
TURNING CIRCLE: 13ft 6in.
MINIMUM NON-SNATCH SPEED: 18-19 m.p.h. in top gear.
WEIGHT PER C.C.: 0.88lb.

Super Profile

THE MOTOR CYCLE, 27 DECEMBER 1951

| ROAD TESTS OF NEW MODELS |

646 c.c. B.S.A. Golden

A Pulse-stirring Vertical Twin Tested Solo

AFTER the war a spate of vertical twins appeared on the British market. These at first were limited to 500 c.c. capacity and there ensued a widespread demand for larger engines, especially from oversea riders and from those requiring machines for sidecar work. The 646 c.c. B.S.A. A10, or Golden Flash, was introduced to meet this demand. It was an immediate success, and in terms of all-round engine performance generally, and in its good torque at medium engine r.p.m. particularly, it far exceeded popular expectations.

The compactness of the engine and gear box—which are wedded on semi-unit-construction lines—makes it difficult to realize that the capacity is as much as 646 c.c. Indeed, the entire machine is clean and trim and, bearing in mind its 425 lb weight, it presents no special difficulties in wheeling it in and out of garages. An idea of its degree of compactness may be judged from the wheelbase, which is less than 55in.

An admirable riding position is provided by the relationship between the seat, footrests and handlebar. The new B.S.A. dual-seat is of ample dimensions and nicely shaped for the maximum comfort of both rider and pillion passenger. Well judged for persons of average stature, the height of the seat furnishes a comfortable knee angle and does not prove unduly high on the occasions when the machine is straddled while at rest, or is being kick-started. Handlebar angle and the height of the footrests are adjustable.

Starting, so far as the test machine was concerned, was not at first as easy as could be desired. Considerable muscular effort was required to rotate the engine, and the mixture strength was weak at smallish throttle openings. The impression was that a throttle slide with rather less cut-away was desirable.

When the engine was cold the starting drill was to flood the carburettor, close the air lever and open the throttle fractionally. Four digs on the kick-starter were the maximum required during the test. When the engine had been running for perhaps a minute, or when, say, a quarter of a mile had been covered, the air slide could be opened fully. Idling had to be on the fast side to be satisfactorily reliable, this because of the patchiness of the carburation mentioned earlier.

Mechanical Quietness

With the engine idling, mechanical noises were all but absent. Piston slap was just audible when the engine was cold, and slight rustling from the overhead-valve rockers could also be heard. In short, however, mechanical quietness is of an extremely high order. Exhaust silencing is most effective and commendably subdued throughout the entire speed range. It is good enough, indeed, to place the Golden Flash right in the front rank in this respect. Induction hiss is completely eliminated by the built-in air filter.

Bottom gear could be engaged noiselessly with the engine idling and the machine stationary. Slightly heavy in operation, the clutch freed perfectly on all occasions, and it was smooth and sweet in taking up the drive. The gear change was well-nigh perfect. Clean and entirely positive upward changes could be made with an easy movement of the right toes. Pedal movement is light and creditably short, and no deliberate slowness in pedal travel was necessary to ensure noiseless gear engagement.

A criticism is that there was considerable gear whine in the indirect ratios, particularly in third. Clean, sweet downward changes could be executed between any pairs of gears just as rapidly as the controls could be operated.

Generally speaking, a small, light machine possessing nippy acceleration forms the most attractive type

Although driven at high speeds throughout the test, the engine unit remained entirely free from oil leaks

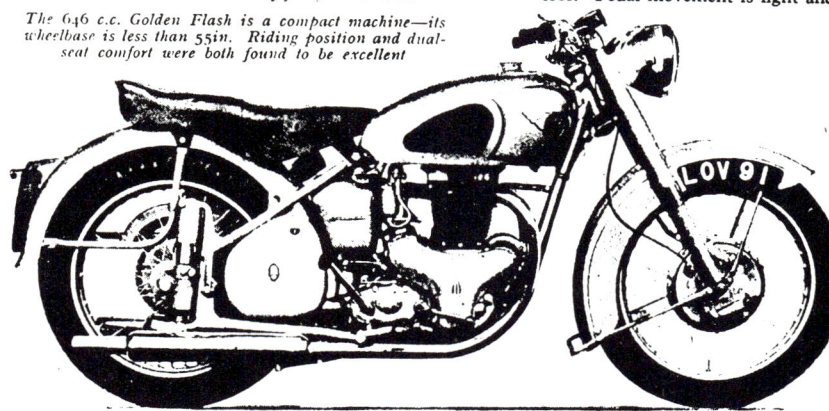

The 646 c.c. Golden Flash is a compact machine—its wheelbase is less than 55in. Riding position and dual-seat comfort were both found to be excellent

The Motor Cycle, 27 December 1951

Flash

nd with Sidecar

Best cruising speed with the B.S.A. single-seat sidecar fitted was judged to be between 55 and 65 m.p.h.

for use in towns and cities. But the A10, though no lightweight, has perfect city manners. Low-speed handling and manoeuvrability are first class; so good, in fact, as to make one forget that the machine is a six-fifty. Low-speed torque is exceptional and the transmission is smooth at low r.p.m. The tendency to pinking was not unduly pronounced, and the response to opening the throttle was full-blooded. Not least important is that the full performance in the indirect gears could be used without fuss from the engine, transmission or exhaust.

But if the Golden Flash has traits which make it attractive in towns and cities, it really comes into its own when being ridden at speed on the open road. Exceptionally high average speeds could be achieved with the minimum of effort on the part of the rider. This was so, not so much because of the machine's over-95 m.p.h. maximum speed, but because of the engine's high mechanical efficiency, even at speeds in excess of those normally used, and its excellent torque at medium revs.

At speeds over 70 m.p.h. there was no marked impression of deliberate hard riding. Only slight increase in throttle opening was necessary to compensate for head-winds or up-gradients. With such colossal engine performance the rider's chosen cruising speed was almost instantaneously regained after a slow-up made necessary by adverse road conditions or traffic. Although consistently high speeds were used throughout the test, the engine remained free from the slightest oil leak. Further, though Pool petrol was used, "running-on" after really hard riding was never experienced. The timing-side exhaust pipe discoloured only faintly, the drive-side one considerably, betraying some degree of carburettor bias.

Handling was very good indeed under all conditions, and the degree of comfort afforded was distinctly outstanding, even judged by the highest present-day standards. The B.S.A. telescopic fork has a long, soft movement which not only absorbs road shocks satisfactorily but, in conjunction with the duplex frame, furnishes, in addition, precise, hair-

Information Panel

SPECIFICATION

ENGINE: 646 c.c. (70 x 84 mm) o.h.v. vertical twin. Fully enclosed valve gear operated by push rods from a single camshaft. Plain bearing big-ends. Mainshafts supported by roller and plain bearings. Compression ratio, 6.5 to 1. Dry-sump lubrication; oil-tank capacity, 4 pints.
CARBURETTOR: Amal; twistgrip throttle control; air-slide operated by handlebar lever. Built-in air-cleaner.
IGNITION AND LIGHTING: Lucas magneto with auto-advance. Separate 45w Lucas dynamo. 7in head lamp. 30-30w head lamp bulb.
TRANSMISSION: B.S.A. four-speed gear box with positive-stop foot control. Solo ratios: Bottom, 11.41 to 1. Second, 7.77 to 1. Third, 5.36 to 1. Top, 4.42 to 1. Sidecar ratios: Bottom, 13.3 to 1. Second, 9.06 to 1. Third, 6.26 to 1. Top, 5.16 to 1. Multi-plate clutch with fabric inserts. Primary chain, $\frac{3}{8}$in duplex in cast-aluminium case. Secondary chain, $\frac{5}{8}$ x $\frac{3}{8}$in. R.p.m at 30 m.p.h. on solo top gear, 1,723, sidecar, 2,012 approx.
FUEL CAPACITY: 4$\frac{1}{4}$ gallons.
TYRES: Dunlop. Front, 3.25 x 19in. Rear, 3.50 x 19in., both studded tread.
BRAKES: 7 x 1$\frac{1}{8}$in rear; 8 x 1$\frac{1}{8}$in front; finger adjusters.
SUSPENSION: B.S.A. telescopic front fork with hydraulic damping. B.S.A. plunger-type rear springing.
WHEELBASE: 54$\frac{1}{2}$in. Ground clearance, 4$\frac{1}{2}$in unladen.
SEAT: B.S.A. dual-seat.
WEIGHT: 425 lb fully equipped and with one gallon of fuel. Complete outfit, 660 lb fully equipped and with one gallon of fuel.
PRICE: Machine only, £175, with Purchase Tax (in Britain only), £223 12s 3d. Extras: Dual-seat, £3; beige finish, £3 (P.T. 16s 8d extra in each case); prop-stand, 15s (P.T. 4s 2d).
ROAD TAX: Solo, £3 15s a year; £1 0s 8d a quarter. Sidecar, £5 a year; £1 7s 7d a quarter.
MAKERS: B.S.A. Cycles, Ltd., Small Heath, Birmingham, 11.
DESCRIPTION: The Motor Cycle, 6 October, 1949, and 19 October, 1950.

SIDECAR

MODEL: B.S.A. 22.47.
CHASSIS: Triangular, with quarter-elliptic springs at rear and twin compression coil springs at front. Four-point attachment.
BODY: Coachbuilt (timber frame, steel panels). Celluloid screen. Folding twill hood. Locker at rear.
PRICE: £61, with Purchase Tax (in Britain only), £77 18s. Beige finish, £3 extra (P.T. 16s 8d extra).

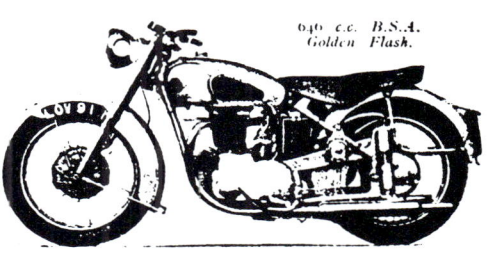

646 c.c. B.S.A. Golden Flash.

PERFORMANCE DATA
(Sidecar figures in brackets)

MEAN MAXIMUM SPEED: Bottom: *42 (*36) m.p.h.
Second: *61 (*51) m.p.h.
Third: 89 (69) m.p.h.
Top: 96 (70) m.p.h.
* Valve float starting.

MEAN ACCELERATION:

	10-30 m.p.h.	20-40 m.p.h.	30-50 m.p.h.
Bottom	2.6 (3.5) secs	3 (—) secs	
Second	4 (4.8) secs	3.2 (4.2) secs	3.6 (4.1) secs
Third	—	5.2 (6.8) secs	5 (6.4) secs
Top	—	— (9.3) secs	6.8 (9) secs

Mean speed at end of quarter-mile from rest: 84 (64) m.p.h.
Mean time to cover standing quarter-mile: 16.8 (20) secs.
PETROL CONSUMPTION: At 30 m.p.h., 72 (50) m.p.g. At 40 m.p.h., 69 (47) m.p.g. At 50 m.p.h., 65 (42) m.p.g. At 60 m.p.h., 59 (37) m.p.g.
BRAKING: From 30 m.p.h. to rest, 29ft (44ft 6in). Surface in each case, dry tar macadam.
TURNING CIRCLE: 12ft 9in.
MINIMUM NON-SNATCH SPEED: 21 (20) m.p.h. in top gear.
WEIGHT PER C.C.: 0.66 lb (1.02 lb).

Super Profile

646 c.c. B.S.A. Golden Flash

line steering. Uncertainty was never felt, no matter how greasy the road surface or how tricky the conditions. On one occasion, indeed, when an attempt was made to take the maximum speed figures, the road was distinctly greasy and there was a strong, gusty cross-wind.

As will be seen from the information panel, the mean maximum speed is given as 96 m.p.h. That figure was obtained at the M.I.R.A. Proving Ground and represents a mean of runs in opposite directions. Average wind speed was 14 m.p.h., with gusts up to 20 m.p.h. The maximum speed recorded down wind—with the air filter connected—was 102.75 m.p.h. and, with it disconnected, 104.5 m.p.h. Maximum speeds up-wind were 86.7 and 87.5 m.p.h. respectively with, and without, the air filter.

Control Positions

When these figures were taken the steering damper was just biting, and the handling was exemplary. Light although the fork movement is, there was no pitching, and there remained a direct "tautness" about the steering that was most satisfying.

In delivery tune, the twistgrip was unduly heavy in operation and a replacement throttle cable and twistgrip had to be fitted to effect a cure. In the main, the controls were well placed for ease of operation, but a criticism in this respect is that it was not possible to set the brake pedal so that the pad lay in the desired position relative to the left footrest.

Used in unison, the brakes provided adequate stopping power even for a machine in the A10's performance class. During the course of the solo test, which included over 500 miles of hard riding, the brakes inevitably came in for severe usage, yet no adjustment was required throughout. Both brakes possessed just the right amount of sponginess to permit hard application. Braking from speed was smooth and progressive, and not the slightest indication of fade, nor any loss of power whatever, was experienced at any time.

At the end of the solo part of the test, the Golden Flash was returned to the factory, where it was fitted with a B.S.A. single-seat sidecar. Alterations to the machine included changing the 42-tooth rear wheel sprocket for one of 49 teeth, and fitting heavier fork springs. At this time, too, the standard 6/4 throttle slide was replaced by a 6/3 (which has 1/16in less cutaway) in order to enrich the mixture at smallish throttle openings.

The result was that patchiness at low speeds disappeared entirely; starting became first-kick instead of third or fourth; acceleration was better than before; and the pick-up was as clean and brisk as could be desired by the most critical enthusiast.

Some 400 miles were covered during the sidecar test. For the greater part of this mileage a 10½-stone passenger was carried and for the remainder of the time the sidecar was empty. In either case the outfit handled magnificently, steering hands-off (with the steering damper just biting) and sweeping round corners with the utmost facility. No more than slight steering-damper friction was required at either high or low speeds. Owing in part to this, the steering was light enough for there to be no driving fatigue, even after a full day in the saddle.

Sidecar Cruising Speed

Best maximum cruising speed with the sidecar fitted appeared to be anything between 55 and 65 m.p.h. At the lower end of the scale the outfit would trickle along in top gear without snatch at speeds of just over 20 m.p.h. Careful handling of the throttle was necessary if, with Pool-quality fuel, pinking was to be avoided during acceleration from this speed. But, bearing in mind the excellent exhaust silencing and the effortless gear change, it was, of course, advisable to make use of the indirect ratios when accelerating from inordinately low speeds.

There was at no time any external indication of over-driving, even though on several occasions the outfit was driven for mile after mile with the throttle against the stop. The riding position for sidecar work was excellent, and no change was required either in footrest position or angle of the grips from the settings used earlier in the test.

Some high-powered machines of the past have been criticized when fitted with sidecars because the brakes have not provided adequate stopping power. No such criticism could be levelled at the B.S.A., however. On the contrary, the sidecar braking figure of 44ft 6in is well above average and would be difficult to better.

Polychromatic Beige

The sidecar itself earned all but full marks. The suspension absorbed road shocks satisfactorily and provided an extremely high degree of comfort for the passenger. Seat and squab are at comfortable angles to one another, and when the hood was raised the interior was cosy and unusually free from draughts. Of the folding type, with a pivoting frame, the hood stows away in a twill envelope when not in use but can be erected in a matter of seconds. A criticism is that during the unusually cold weather prevailing when the test was carried out, the screen provided rather insufficient side protection.

Both the machine and the sidecar were luxuriously finished in polychromatic beige. The tank finish was fully polychromatic, with no chromium plating, and with red lining on the top and side surfaces. The quality of the Golden Flash finish as a whole was unusually high for any class of road vehicle. It is a machine which will undoubtedly do as much to enhance the reputation of the marque as any other B.S.A. produced in the last 20 years.

The 646 c.c. engine, neat and well-proportioned, appears to be no larger than the average five-hundred unit

MOTOR CYCLING SPORTS MODEL ROAD TESTS

The 646 c.c. Vertical-twin o.h.v.

B.S.A. "ROAD ROCKET"

Impressions of a Potent Small Heath Product

DESIGNED as a road-going solo with just that little extra in the way of speed and specification luxury likely to make it a dollar earner, the B.S.A. "Road Rocket" well fulfilled its original purpose in the export field and made a mid-season debut on the home market recently. Almost at once B.S.A.s responded to a request that *Motor Cycling* should carry out a road test of this reputedly most powerful of the Small Heath twins and, therefore, this article becomes the first test report of the "Road Rocket" to appear in a British motorcycling journal.

Basically, the machine is a highly developed version of the 646 c.c. A10, featuring an aluminium-alloy cylinder head, "Nimonic 80" exhaust valves, a toughened, high-duty crankshaft and high-compression pistons giving a ratio of 8 : 1. For this power unit the makers record a conservative figure of 40 b.h.p. at 6,000 r.p.m. Listed with a 4.53 top gear as standard, the machine is said officially to have a maximum speed in the region of 105 m.p.h., which, again, would appear to be a modest claim.

Tested under almost ideal weather conditions, the "Road Rocket" gave the initial impression that a slightly higher gear-ratio could have been used; indeed, the tester was pleasantly surprised that, at the quoted maximum rate of r.p.m., the speedometer needle was just passing the "ton" and that there was a degree of power still in hand. Actually, on several timed test runs, slightly more than 110 m.p.h. was speedo-recorded.

It is true to say, however, that such speeds cannot necessarily be regarded as a day-to-day certainty. On the other hand, a more enduring feature is the fact that one can

(Right) Essential with such a machine the rev.-counter, matching the speedometer, is carried just where the rider's eye can read it with the minimum deflection from the view ahead. Note also the steering lock keyhole.

(Below) A picture to delight the eye of any motorcycle enthusiast—the 650 c.c. o.h.v. twin engine of the A10RR.

TESTER'S ROAD REPORT

Maximum Speeds in:—

			Time from Standing Start
Top Gear (Ratio 4·53 to 1)	109 m.p.h.	6,200 r.p.m.	42·5 secs
Third Gear (Ratio 5·48 to 1)	88 m.p.h.	6,300 r.p.m.	20 secs
Second Gear (Ratio 7·9 to 1)	67 m.p.h.	6,500 r.p.m.	12 secs

Speeds over measured Quarter Mile:—

Flying Start 108·4 m.p.h.   Standing Start 58·06 m.p.h.

Braking Figures On DRY TARMACADAM Surface, from 30 m.p.h.:—

Both Brakes 28 ft.   Front Brake 33 ft.   Rear Brake 72 ft.

Fuel Consumption:—

30 m.p.h. 90 m.p.g.   40 m.p.h. 70 m.p.g.   50 m.p.h. 50 m.p.g.

Super Profile

MOTOR CYCLING SPORTS MODEL ROAD TESTS

Under suitable conditions, any private owner could simulate the riding positions with which the speeds recorded here were obtained.

rely on the "Road Rocket" for sustained high average speeds irrespective of the "ceiling." This B.S.A. model, designated the A10RR, could be cruised without signs of fatigue at speeds between 95-100 m.p.h.—given suitable road conditions, of course. But it is the kind of motorcycle which a foreign-touring enthusiast would find delightful to own. It would be invaluable as a means of rapid, yet rock-steady, transport on journeys over the straight and relatively traffic-free *routes nationales* or *autobahnen* of Europe. Nearer home, the chief appeal of the "Road Rocket" lies, not so much in its top-speed capabilities, which, alas, cannot always be fully used, but in acceleration qualities.

Off the mark like a shot in bottom gear, the model has an acceleration curve that rises steeply and consistently, there being no sign of "flat spots" in the carburation provided by the Amal 10TT9 instrument. The gears are well selected and the gear-change excellent. As might be expected, with an 8 : 1 c.r., tick-over and slow running were a little erratic but, by discreet use of the manual ignition control, the tendency towards uneven firing at low r.p.m. could be minimized. When once on the move the control could be advanced fully and, unless pinking was provoked by intentional ham-handedness, the power build-up could be used efficiently right up to maximum speed.

Although listed as an extra, the Smiths rev.-counter fitted to the test machine was regarded as an almost essential complement to the speedometer, particularly in view of the engine's willingness to soar up above manufacturer's recommended maximum. At the top-speed second- and third-gear readings recorded on the graph, valve-float was *just* audible.

Generally Handling

Handling, by which is meant steering and the general ease of riding, earned full marks and there was nothing which could be "blacked" from a comfort point of view. The action of the suspension units, front and rear, was smooth but there was the sound of metallic impact somewhere in the front fork assembly on occasions when a ridge or depression happened to be struck at speed and, apparently, at a certain angle. The sound occurred only two or three times in the course of several hundred miles and did not appear to be a symptom of any serious fault. Criticism could legitimately be levelled also at the efficiency of the rear brake. Both brakes applied together produced an excellent stopping figure and the forward brake, which was used for about 80% of the stopping work, proved to be completely reliable and fade-free. Operation of the back "stopper" produced a spongy reaction which did not improve as the test proceeded.

High-speed performance does not usually go hand-in-hand with economy in the amount of fuel consumed and the A10RR, with its T.T.-type carburetter carrying a 340 main jet, could hardly be an exception to this general rule. In fact, first experience, which comprised riding in city, suburban and high-speed main road environs—good, mixed going—a 175-mile journey served to empty completely the four-gallon tank that had been filled at the works before starting out. And that meant an average of about 43 m.p.g.! But like many high-performance models with a high compression ratio, the "Road Rocket" acquitted itself well in the fixed speed tests.

Fittings, generally, were of good quality and substantial; full marks went to the dual seat, correctly angled to give comfort in conditions produced by hard acceleration and braking. The seat blended well with the lines of the tank, the sides of which are flattened at knee level for the same reason. A centre stand was fitted but seldom used because of the existence of a much more easily operated prop-stand. This, wrongly in the opinion of the tester, came under the heading of an extra. The chromed hand-rail behind the seat added to appearance value and provided satisfactory handhold for the passenger or while manœuvring the machine.

Pillion foot rests were well positioned for their purpose which was not that of providing a species of alternative racing rests to suit a racing poise. That scheme was not practicable, at least not to a rider of the stature of either of *Motor Cycling*'s men in the Midlands, and for this reason (amongst others) all the graphed speeds were recorded with the tester normally seated, if crouching a little so as to present minimum frontal resistance.

A newcomer with good and not-far-distant ancestry, the "Road Rocket" assuredly will add to both home and overseas prestige of British-made motorcycles.

BRIEF SPECIFICATION

Engine: 646 c.c. twin-cylinder four-stroke; bore 70 mm. by stroke 84 mm.; cast-iron cylinder; light-alloy head; overhead valves; push-rod operated; C.R. 8 : 1. Claimed b.h.p. 40 at 6,000 r.p.m.; Amal carburetter, type 10TT9, 1 1/16-in. choke. 340 main jet.

Transmission: Four-speed gearbox; positive-stop footchange; ratios, 4.53, 5.48, 7.96 and 11.68 : 1; primary drive by chain ½ in. by .305 in.; final drive by chain ⅝ in. by ⅜ in.

Frame: Welded duplex tubular cradle type.

Wheels: WM2-19 rims, carrying Dunlop tyres; 3.25-in. by 19-in. ribbed front, 3.50-in by 19-in. Universal rear; full-width alloy hubs; incorporate 7-in. brakes at front and rear.

Lubrication: Dry-sump lubrication with double gear type oil pump; oil tank 5½ pints capacity.

Electrical Equipment: Lucas magneto with manual ignition control lever; 6v. dynamo with C.V.C. unit; prefocus 7-in. diameter headlamp with pilot light; 12 a.h. battery; stop/tail lamp with reflector; electric horn and dipswitch.

Suspension: Telescopic front forks of B.S.A. design, controlled by hydraulic damping; rear springing by swinging fork; movement controlled by Girling units with hydraulic damping; spindle adjustment by means of abutment screws.

Tank: Welded steel fuel tank, of 4 gal. capacity.

Dimensions: Wheelbase, 56 in.; ground clearance, 6 in.; unladen seat height, 30 in.; dry weight, 418 lb.

Finish: Black stove enamel, red tank with chrome panels; mudguards, exhaust system, wheel rims, handlebars and other bright parts chrome plated.

General Equipment: Full kit of tools; tyre pump; 120 m.p.h. Smiths speedometer; pillion footrests; steering damper, steering head lock.

Price: £217 10s. plus £52 4s. P.T.=£269 14s. (total, with extras, £279 15s. 8d.).

Annual Tax: £3 15s.; quarterly, £1 0s. 8d.

Makers: B.S.A. Motor Cycles, Ltd., Small Heath, Birmingham, 11.

Extras (fitted to test model): Rev. counter, prop-stand, chrome hand-rail.

Super Profile

OWNER'S VIEW

When riding a BSA A7 or A10, one re-discovers the traditional style of motorcycling and wonders just what has really improved over the years since the last A10 left the BSA Small Heath Factory.

The BSA twin still has much to offer as a tourer or everyday practical mount, giving good fuel economy, with adequate performance. The low-speed pull and flexible engine make town riding a joy. As long as owner-riders exploit these virtues, the BSA A7/A10 will continue to be seen on the roads. Wherever you go with your machine it will turn the heads of interested onlookers and you will come across many inquisitive passers-by.

I was always attracted by that solid looking engine, accentuated by the three-lobed outer timing cover. The first time I'd ever been on a motorcycle was as a first year engineering apprentice. I took a pillion ride on a workmate's A10 Road Rocket. The rider gave the machine full throttle as we roared on through town and rural lane. I was completely taken by sheer exhilaration and this lasting experience made me into a staunch BSA follower.

A fellow club member had a late swinging arm A10 Golden Flash languishing forlornly in an outbuilding. When it became 'surplus to requirements' I raided the bank and joined the gallant A10 ranks, embarking on the long process of restoration.

The bike was caked in filth. The exhaust, seat and numerous cycle fittings were missing. When the engine was stripped down it revealed a worn-out camshaft and cam-follower set. The crankshaft sludge-trap was solid and required drilling out!

After three years of haggling over replacement parts at autojumbles and many hours spent restoring and rebuilding, my Golden Flash took to the road one clear August evening. My aim had been to build a basically standard bike without going to the extremes of exact original detail. My A10 will work for its living and one day it may pull a sidecar to enable the family to enjoy a day out.

I immediately found the A10 very quiet to ride, with no disconcerting noises. There is a vibration period at about 50-55mph that makes one feel as if the engine had reached its peak. Then from 55mph it seems to find second breath, and pulls smoothly onwards, being more reassuring at a constant 65-70mph. Handling is good and cornering doesn't require any shifting about in the saddle. It gives me a return of over 60mpg on a steady run.

In retrospect I'm glad I bought a dilapidated machine and repaired, restored and replaced every part, This enabled me to become intimate with the workings of the A10. I was very impressed with the general standard of engineering and workmanship.

Dave Hurson of Coventry has had a wide experience of A7 and A10 twins, both plunger and swinging arm types, in either solo or combination form. In 1979 he completed a lengthy restoration of a 1952 A7 Star Twin. It was a pleasure to listen to his views and stories concerning his past and present BSA twins. This is how he answered a number of questions, giving some useful advice for other owners:

OW: Why are you so interested in the BSA A7 and A10 twins?
DH: I had a number of BSAs starting with Bantams, then a B31, until I worked my way up to an A10 Rocket. The spares were always cheap and easy to get although I never had any problems with the numerous bikes I'd owned. I developed a sort of allegiance to BSA and in particular to the A7.
OW: When and why did you buy your A7 Star Twin?
DH: After some years without a BSA I fancied doing up a plunger A7 or A10. Having owned a lot of other makes, including my present BMW, I was still longing for an old BSA Twin. A friend told me about an A7 Star Twin that was for sale a few years ago. I was more interested in a plunger A7 than any of the other versions. I reckon it to be a lot smoother and easier to ride than the A10.
OW: What condition was the A7 in?
DH: It was a rusty frame and a box of bits! I paid about £5 for it. A lot of parts were missing and what remained of the engine was completely dismantled.
OW: You obviously had a lot of repair and renovation work to do. What advice would you give someone else facing the same problems?
DH: Well, they're easy bikes to work on and put together, but there is a lot of it! It would be better to find a more complete bike, but the A7 Star Twin was too good to pass by. If you are rebuilding or renovating one of these machines, and let's say it's in a better state than mine was, you mustn't start taking everything to pieces, otherwise it all gets mislaid. Concentrate on one thing at a time. Also, you have to decide how far you want to go with the rebuild. You may just want to get something on the road as soon as possible or you could aim at getting the bike back to full original condition. This can take a very long time and be expensive, though very satisfying when completed.

Super Profile

OW: Have you experienced difficulty in obtaining any parts? If so, what solutions did you find?
DH: Some parts for my A7 were very difficult to find. There seems to be a lot more 650cc stuff available. A new pair of con-rods took a long time to find and the correct type of petrol tank required some searching. Unbelievably, the tank badges for the Star Twin are probably one of the rarest items of all. Having owned a few of these bikes years ago I knew quite a few places that still had a lot of BSA spares. Autojumbles are one of the best sources of parts. Being in an organised club also helps by contacting various members and organising swaps.
OW: What kind of performance and handling does the bike have?
DH: It's very enjoyable to ride. After riding the BMW it feels very light. I've opened it up to see what it can do. It managed about 85 to 90mph. At that speed it get a bit lumpy! Apart from a slight vibration band at 55mph it's nice, and for a vertical twin, smooth. The handling takes some getting used to, especially cornering. With plungers on the back it tends to wallow a little. Brakes are good, very predictable.
OW: Is your A7 in regular use? If so, is it practical and are the running costs high?
DH: I use it mainly for club events although I've done some long distance touring in Europe, the BSA Rally in Holland, the F.I.M. Rally in Switzerland. The A7 is insured with my other bike. There are one or two good insurance schemes available these days that are sympathetic to older bikes. Overall I'd say that yes, it is practical to run; fuel consumption is about 70mpg.
OW: Has your bike won any prizes in concours or similar events?
DH: Yes, a bottle of whisky at a rally in Scotland! Somewhere near Peebles.
OW: Do you belong to any clubs? If so, do you think it helps?
DH: I've been in the BSA Owners Club for some years now. I was also a member of an all make club in Coventry. It certainly helps; without the BSA Club there wouldn't be much to do. I like going to rallies, making contacts with other A7 owners, buying and selling spares, that sort of thing.
OW: Is there a particular specialist whom you found useful?
DH: Some of the places that I bought spares from have since gone, but C and D Autos in Birmingham provided many parts.
OW: How would you sum up the enjoyment you get from your A7 Star Twin.
DH: It's eveything I had hoped it to be. It really came up to expectations. I always look forward to taking it out somewhere. The model is a bit scarce now and it's the identical type and year to the ones that won the Maudes Trophy in 1952, so it gathers a lot of interest along the way.
OW: What advice would you give potential owners of an A7 or A10.
DH: Go ahead and get one! There's no real problems. Let the bike be whatever you want it to be. You don't have to go mad to make sure every nut and bolt is the exact original. These bikes are a viable form of everyday transport; the best part about the whole thing is riding them.

No other British motorcycle captured the public's imagination as much as the A10 Rocket Gold Star, the final development of the series. It had come a long way from the first A7 of 1946. The Rocket Gold Star has created something of a legend and is shrouded in mystery. I contacted Alan Lightfoot, who has owned one for many years. Here Alan answers my questions and gives an interesting insight into the Rocket Gold Star.

OW: Why are you so interested in the Rocket Gold Star?
AL: I have always liked BSAs and I was attracted to the Rocket Gold Star because of its sporty appeal.
OW: When and why did you buy your Rocket Gold Star?
AL: I bought it in 1966; someone was selling it at the right price.
OW: What condition was it in?
AL: The bike was in reasonable condition but it had been standing in a shed for over a year.
OW: What repair and renovation work has been done?
AL: The bike has been completely rebuilt three times. For the third time I rebuilt it to original condition, I've had the frame resprayed, tank repaired, many parts re-chromed.
OW: What is the best way of tackling the renovation work?
AL: Don't be in a hurry to get things done and if you come across anything that you aren't sure of then don't be afraid to ask the experts. Don't take short cuts for the sake of a little bit of time or money.
OW: Would it have been more economical to have bought a machine in better or worse condition than yours initially?
AL: At the time I bought the bike I don't think I considered that. Nowadays I would purchase an original machine in any condition.
OW: Have you experienced difficulties in obtaining any parts? What solution did you find in locating parts?
AL: The cycle parts are always the most difficult bits to find. The best solution I found was attending autojumbles, auctions and, failing this, pattern parts are available.
OW: What kind of performance and handling does the Rocket Gold Star have?
AL: I've always been pleased with the performance of the engine and the close ratio RRT2 gearbox, but the handling isn't too good on rough roads.
OW: Is your bike in regular use? How practical is it and are the running costs high?
AL: The bike is not in daily use, I just go to rallies etc., when the sun is on my back!
OW: Has your bike won any prizes in concours or similar events?
AL: I won the best classic bike award at a recent open day organised by the Velocette Owners Club.
OW: Is there an owners club, are

Super Profile

you a member?
AL: I used to be a member of the Gold Star Owners Club.
OW: Is there a specialist whom you found particularly useful?
AL: There are two people whom I found equally helpful and both provide an excellent return of post service. They are George Prew and Ken Gardner.
OW: How would you sum up the enjoyment you get from your Rocket Gold Star?
AL: I have always enjoyed riding the Rocket Gold Star, it is very economical in comparison to present day machinery and from experience it has always been very dependable.
OW: What advice would you give to potential owners of the Rocket Gold Star?
AL: If you are lucky enough to locate one (be careful, there's a lot about that aren't genuine) hang on to it! Not only do you have a good investment but a very good British motorcycle.

Super Profile

BUYING

The A7 and A10 models enjoyed a long and prolific production run. Spares for the basic models do not present any problems in obtaining, but some cycle parts such as fuel tanks, tool boxes and mudguards can be scarce and require a more diligent search. Thankfully, quite a lot of BSA twins are still in everyday use and many new durable engine parts are currently being manufactured to meet the demand. Compared to buying a brand new (and almost certainly foreign) machine, a BSA twin can be a worthwhile alternative. They are very reliable and easy to maintain and, of course, provide a sense of attachment and pride, something that is unfortunately missing with modern motorcycles.

The overall design had very few failings and was generally free of faults. The BSA type six-spring clutch was sensitive to the amount of oil contained in the chaincase, and the margin between slip and drag was small. Many owners fitted cork inserts to the friction plates, in place of fabric, and discarded the pressed steel cover to allow the unit to run freely in oil. Another method, particularly applied to the swinging arm models, was to fit a Triumph type clutch, using a purchasable conversion sleeve. Gear changing can be notchy and neutral difficult to find, not helped by the erratic six-spring clutch. Owners found it easier to obtain neutral before coming to a stop.

The brakes are hard pushed to meet modern traffic conditions. It is a matter of opinion amongst owner-riders as to whether the older half-widths hubs were better than the alloy or later cast-iron full width types. The full width rear brakes were operated by a cable that was inefficient and gave a rather 'spongy' feel. All brakes are fairly good at low speed but do tend to fade under high demand. Many late swinging arm owners fitted a Triumph type twin-leading shoe front brake.

The engines had a reputation for quiet running, though alloy cylinder head models do accentuate a certain amount of noise. They are also reasonably oil tight. The one-piece rocker inspection caps could weep oil if the mating faces were marked. The camshaft mounted breather sleeve had a cork washer that was supplied in various thicknesses. If too much axial clearance was allowed, or the washer was worn, then this could give a very oily engine. Some distraught owners on finding a large pool of oil underneath the bike found that the fault lay with the anti-syphon ball valve held off its seat by a speck of dirt. The remedy was to remove the sump plate and prod the steel ball with a piece of wire. Oil consumption should not be less than 250-300 miles per pint.

Lighting and ignition systems were very simple and common with other contemporary machines. The 6 volt lighting gave enough illumination for a safe speed of about 55mph at night. It is becoming more popular these days to convert to a 12 volt system.

The biggest enemy to the electrical equipment was vibration. So many failures were due to poor and erratic connections. On an old machine it pays to have a complete re-wire. New wiring harnesses are still easy to obtain.

As far as values are concerned, the models from the opposite ends of the range can be expected to hold high prices. An early long-stroke A7 is now a very rare sight on the road. Spares for these machines are the hardest to find. Whilst the final version of the A10, the Rocket Gold Star, is a certain collectors' piece and must surely be one of the most sought-after British motorcycles. Both these machines are really for the experts. Many enthusiasts uprated stock A10s to Rocket Gold Star specification. A genuine example can be identified by having a frame number prefix containing 'A10'; all other 650s shared the same frames with the 500cc models and were stamped A7.

Overall, the ordinary plunger and swinging arm models fall into the same price bracket. Both types have their local enthusiasts. Few parts were interchangeable between plunger and swinging arm twins, therefore, A7 and A10 owners tend to divide into two factions.

Throughout the history of the twins, the A7 was never regarded as the poor relation. In fact many riders favoured the smoother and more docile performance of the 500. We also must remember that after such a passage of time so many machines have been altered, modified, or received replacement engines. The type of owner-rider buying an A7/A10 varied as much as the machines did. Many BSA twins started life as a family man's work-a-day transport and finished up as a motorway sprinter. BSA too were known to deviate from the standard specification described in the catalogue. As mass producers interested in meeting production targets, some corners were cut short and anomalies in fittings, colours and equipment did occur. All these facts have to be taken into account, especially if the intention is to build a machine back to 'as factory' or to enter a club concours.

Buying a machine in running order or one that is the proverbial 'box of bits' will require about the same financial outlay. This depends on how far the intended restoration is taken. It is not worth spending a large amount of money on a dismantled machine and such can be very deceptive. Unless you are familiar with the A7/A10 it is difficult to assess the entirety of a dismantled bike.

In finding a suitable A7 or A10, it's worth reading the various weekly motorcycling newspapers and magazines to get some grasp of the current prices being asked. These values do, however, tend to be speculative and even untidy machines command a hopeful price. This is where it pays to be a member of a club. A lot of buying and selling goes on at club meetings and enthusiasts are more likely to trade with one another at reasonable prices. The various autojumbles held throughout the country are another good source of purchase. Be prepared to haggle with the vendor; many traders would sooner see an exchange for cash rather than transport a hefty motorcycle across the country. Auctions can go from one extreme to another. Whilst it is known for absolute bargains to be found, it is more likely that the final bid will go beyond proportions as excited buyers make rash and excessive bids. Auctions do have a bad reputation for withdrawing items that don't meet the expected price. Also, look into the most unlikely places such as shop window small ads. Talk to people about their past motorcycling days; so many motorcycles are still to be found hidden away in garden sheds and outbuildings. Finally, it's surprising just how much attention a BSA can draw when you go for a ride. Absolute strangers will stop to talk to you and reminisce. Actually owning a BSA twin can lead to further acquisitions!

Super Profile

CLUBS, SPECIALISTS, BOOKS

Clubs

There is no club that caters exclusively for BSA A7 and A10 twins but the **BSA Owners Club** has many rider-enthusiasts within its ranks. A7 and A10 models indeed form the backbone of its membership. The BSAOC has over 30 branches throughout Britain and numerous overseas associated clubs and branches. As well as providing a full social and rally programme, information relating to technical and historical matters can be obtained. The BSAOC can also provide data on machine identification and registration dating. For full details contact:-

**Alistair Fitzgerald,
12 Plant Lane,
Long Eaton,
Nottingham.**

Owners of A10 Rocket Gold Star machines may be interested in joining the Gold Star Owners Club. The address to contact is:-

**John Gardner,
23 Wellington Close,
Dibden Purlieu,
Southampton.**

It is worth mentioning that owners of machines that are 25 years or more old are eligible to join the Vintage Motor Cycle Club. For full details contact:-

**Jim Hammant,
'Red Oaks',
Mill Lane,
Lower Shiplake,
Henley-on-Thames,
Oxon,
RG9 3LN**

Specialists

It is worth reading the various popular motorcycling magazines for names and addresses of individuals and companies that specialise in A7 and A10 spares. The magazines, *'Classic Bike'* and *'The Classic Motor Cycle'* will prove most help. Here are a few leading specialists that will supply A7/A10 spares and literature:-

**C & D Autos,
1193-1199 Warwick Road,
Acocks Green,
Birmingham,
B27 6BY,
England.
(021-706 2902)**
Excellent stocks of BSA A7/A10 spares.

**Bri-Tie Motorcycles,
1, Armstrong Street,
Swindon,
Wilts,
England.
(0793 31518)**
Excellent stocks of BSA A7/A10 spares. Also has good restoration facilities such as stove enamelling and chroming. May also provide good quality literature.

**Lewis and Sons
(Weybridge) Ltd,
51, Church Street,
Weybridge,
Surrey,
England.
(0932 42210)**
Have huge stocks of genuine BSA spares.

**SRM Engineering,
A20 Penarth Dock,
Penarth,
South Glamorgan,
CF6 1XZ
Wales
(0222 708132)**
Specialists in improving A7/A10 engines. Full engineering facilities, manufacture and fit timing side main bearing conversions.

**R.J. Motorcycles,
18-20, Hotel Street,
Coalville,
Leicestershire.**
Always have many secondhand spares in stock.

Owners of A10 Rocket Gold Star machines will find the following specialists particularly useful:-

**George Prew,
Mill House,
Barkway,
Nr. Royston,
Herts.
Tel: Barkway 763**

**K & J Gardner,
Wolford Heath
Shipston-on-Stour
Warwickshire,
Tel: 0608 84306**

Books

A7/A10 literature can be summarised as follows:-

Original BSA Workshop Manuals and Owners Handbooks.
Genuine or reprinted BSA publications may be purchased from the specialists listed previously. Good quality xerox copies are usually available from **Bruce Main-Smith Retail, PO Box 20, Leatherhead, Surrey, England.**

Pitmans Book of the BSA twin (A7 and A10) by W.C. Haycraft. Two editions and three reprints from 1960 to 1972. All out of print but often found at autojumbles and auctions. Contains concise servicing details.

BSA A7 and A10 twins Owners Workshop Manual by Jeff Clew. Obtainable from **Haynes Publishing Group, Sparkford, Yeovil, Somerset, BA22 7JJ, England.**
Features a step by step guide to overhauling a BSA twin, with photographs. Covers all models.

BSA twins and triples by Roy Bacon.
Published in 1980 by **Osprey Publishing Ltd, 12-14 Long Acre, London WC2E 9LP, England.**
Contains a full history, detailed specifications and listing of engine/frame numbers. Also has many excellent photographs.

British Motorcycles since 1950. Volume 2. by Steve Wilson. Published by **Patrick Stephens Ltd, Bar Hill, Cambridge, CB3 8EL, England.**
Volume 2 is almost entirely of BSA motorcycles. Contains an in-depth study of the Birmingham Small Arms Co since 1950. A full detailed account of the A7/A10 twins is included, with a useful section on production changes and specifications and engine/frame numbers.

Super Profile

PHOTO GALLERY

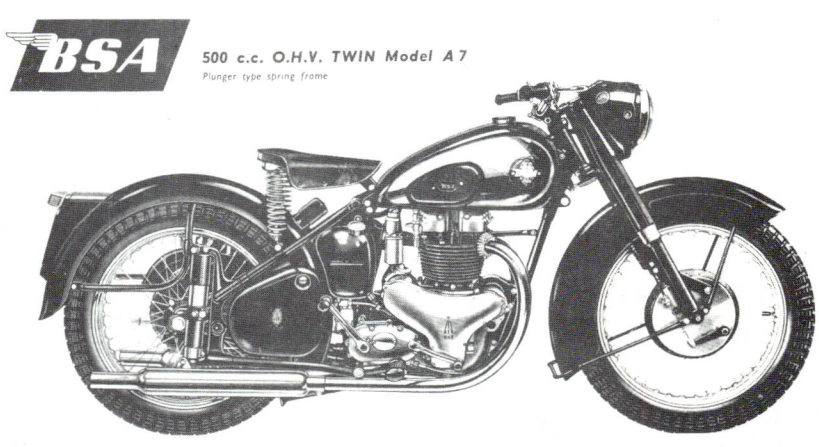

1. The 1954 497cc Plunger A7. Good brakes and easy for town riding. The round piled arms tank badge was newly introduced for this year. Plunger A7s were available until 1955. Plunger A10s lingered on until 1958.

2. The first swinging arm rear suspension A10 Golden Flash as it appeared in 1954. The drawing shows a butterfly type filler cap for the oil tank, which was seldom used.

3. The 1962 A10 Super Rocket. Visual differences between A7 and A10 variants are difficult to spot. The A7 had 7 cylinder barrel fins, the A10 had 8.

4. The 1954 A7 Star Twin racing machine. They took first and second places at Daytona ahead of three 500cc Gold Star singles!

5. The last great fling, the 1962-63 A10 Rocket Gold Star.

Super Profile

6. 'You turn left at Marble Arch, then it's the Sahara desert!' Bob Forrest-Webb (in arrowed sleeve jacket) explains the route to Geoff Monty. Ron Spillman (with glasses) looks on. The three journeyed to the Southern rim of the Sahara desert and back in January 1960. They covered 4500 miles in just two weeks. The outfit is a standard A10 Golden Flash hitched to a Watsonian sidecar.

7. A10s could go anywhere! Even across the Tadamait plateau in the middle of the Sahara desert.

8. A 1960 650cc A10 Golden Flash. It was perhaps the last of the classical British motorcycles with its pre-unit construction, magneto ignition, dynamo lighting and a cast-iron cylinder head.

9. The final version of the A10 Golden Flash had this nacelle headlamp/fork-shroud style as well as slim valanced mudguards and convex toolbox with matching oiltank. The machine weighed a hefty 430 lbs (dry).

10. The A7/A10 series was one of the most well-thought-out designs from BSA. The home mechanic, armed with just a modest array of tools, can keep the machine in top condition.

11. Although this A10 is shown on its centre-stand, a side stand was provided. It was clamped to the frame just below the primary chaincase.

Super Profile

12

13

14

15

16

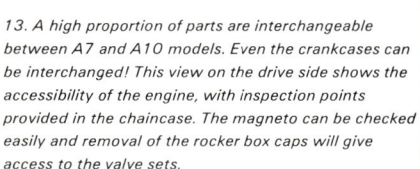
17

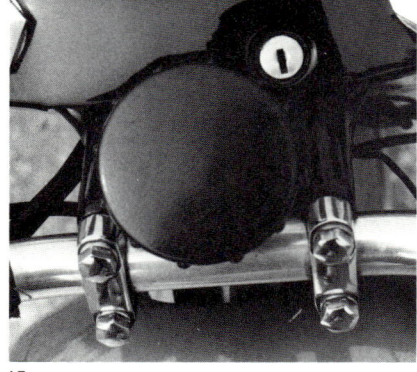

18

12. The outer timing cover characterises the A7 and A10. Removal of the cover will reveal a chain drive to the dynamo (mounted in front of the engine) and also give access to the magneto auto advance-retard unit. The feed and return oil pipes can be seen taking a route under the gearbox. On the earlier plunger-framed models on which the gearbox was bolted directly to the engine, the pipes ran over the gearbox.

13. A high proportion of parts are interchangeable between A7 and A10 models. Even the crankcases can be interchanged! This view on the drive side shows the accessibility of the engine, with inspection points provided in the chaincase. The magneto can be checked easily and removal of the rocker box caps will give access to the valve sets.

14. Rider's eye view. Ammeter on the left and lighting switch on the right. The Smiths Chronometric speedometer features an odometer and tripmeter. The latter can be 'zeroed' by turning a small knob that extends downwards from the meter. A steering damper was fitted on all models. It was a relic from earlier days though sidecar users may have had some use for it. The steering lock was first fitted in 1956.

15. The nacelle-type headlamp unit has a Lucas ammeter mounted on the left. The chrome ring with lozenge shaped flashes (one each side) adds the finishing touches. The small screw on top of the nacelle will release the headlamp rim for bulb replacement.

16. On late models, the horn was fitted inside the nacelle, screwed to the bottom fork yoke. That 7 inch headlamp is a Lucas MCF700P item. Note the chrome bezel fitted underneath the lighting switch.

17. The handlebars are held in place with two clamps directly onto the top fork yoke. This model is fitted with semi-western type handlebars.

18. Ball-ended handlebars were only fitted to some American export models and the headlamp dipper with combined horn button shown here is an accessory. It was commonly fitted as a replacement for the original equipment.

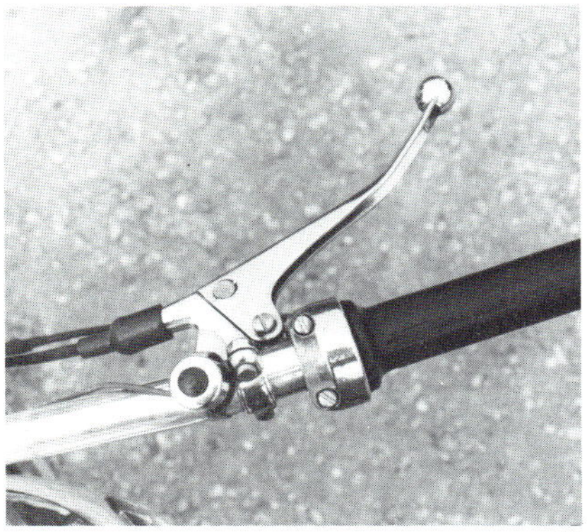

Super Profile

19. The button switch connects to an earth stud on the magneto, cutting the ignition when pressed. The ball-ended lever is a more modern feature but a popular modification.

20. The front mudguard is supported upon brackets which in turn are clamped to the lower fork legs. The lower mudguard stay can be used to support the machine during front wheel removal!

21. 1958 on, cast-iron full width hubs are characterised by having straight-pull spokes. The brake backplate is alloy. It has a cast-in slot to locate with the fork leg. Quite a variety of cable types were used; this machine has a soldered on fork, most had a loose shackle.

22. The front mudguard stay can be detached here and used to prop up the machine for front wheel removal.

23. The wheel spindle is located by a split clamp bolted to the lower fork leg. The outer brake cable is seated in a cup formed in the brake shoe pivot. Oil capacity for each fork leg is $\frac{3}{8}$ Imp. pint.

24. The front engine mounting consists of two fabricated brackets which also act as a cover for the dynamo. The dynamo clamp can be seen.

25. The swinging arm frame models have true pre-unit construction. The power unit is held by a system of engine plates whilst the separate gearbox is pivoted at the bottom, with a drawbolt at the top to enable adjustment of the primary chain tension. On plunger-framed models the gearbox was bolted directly to the engine; primary chain tension was then achieved by an adjustable slipper. The oil pressure relief valve can be seen in front of the timing cover.

Super Profile

26

27

26. Removal of the elliptical gearbox cover will permit clutch adjustment and facilitate topping up with oil to the recommended level. There is a plug at the rear of the gearbox that serves as an oil level check. The gear lever is located upon a serrated shaft with a clamping bolt whilst the kickstart lever has a cotter pin. The cotter pin shown here is positioned the wrong way round and the kick starter rubber is missing. Unless specified, a rigid type kickstart lever was normally fitted to A10 Golden Flash models.

27. Behind the gear lever, the oil supply/return pipes can be seen. The uppermost pipe is the return line back to the oil tank and the lower pipe is the engine feed. The crankcase bosses are stamped R and F to avoid confusion. The speedometer drive cable can be seen. It is driven by a worm gear from the gearbox layshaft. BSA supplied various alternative worm gears for non-standard gear clusters, or if a smaller engine sprocket had been fitted for sidecar use.

28. The gearbox drawbolt also has a serrated collar, for locking purposes. Note the grease nipple for the clutch operating lever mechanism.

28

29. The clutch cable fitted to this machine has an adjuster at the gearbox. This was normally featured on earlier models. By 1960 the adjustment was provided at the handlebar lever, with a plain brass ferrule located in the gearbox cable lug.

30. By 1958, BSA discarded the inner pressed steel clutch cover and revised the method of clutch adjustment, hence the slotted cap provided in the chaincase cover. It was retained for 1960 on machines fitted with a 4-spring clutch. The upper cap permits chain inspection. Obscured by the exhaust is a combined drain/level standpipe screwed into the underside of the cover.

29

30

Super Profile

31. Restyled, wide-finned cylinder barrels were introduced with the swinging arm models in 1954. They were also fitted to the later plunger A10 models too. Even though the A10 and A7 cylinder heads differed in detail, it was known for them to be interchanged (albeit erroneously) without difficulty.

32. The dynamo end cap is retained by a single screw. Removal of the cap will give access to the brush gear. The engine number stamped at the crankcase mouth shows that this machine is fitted with a DA series motor, the final version. One exterior feature of this engine is a $\frac{1}{2}$ inch thick cylinder barrel flange. Earlier engines had a $\frac{3}{8}$ inch thick flange. This modification was necessary to keep pace with higher compression ratios and performance.

33. Amal Monobloc-type carburettors were first fitted in 1955. The drip tray is missing, as is the Tufnol spacer between cylinder manifold and carburettor. The Jubilee clip fitted to the airbox rubber is a non-standard fitting!

34. The Lucas K2F magneto is held to the timing side crankcase with 3 nuts. The lower nut is a special extended type. Two petrol taps are provided, one to act as a 'reserve'. The pointed lug welded to the frame is for a tyre inflator, standard equipment on every machine.

Super Profile

35

36

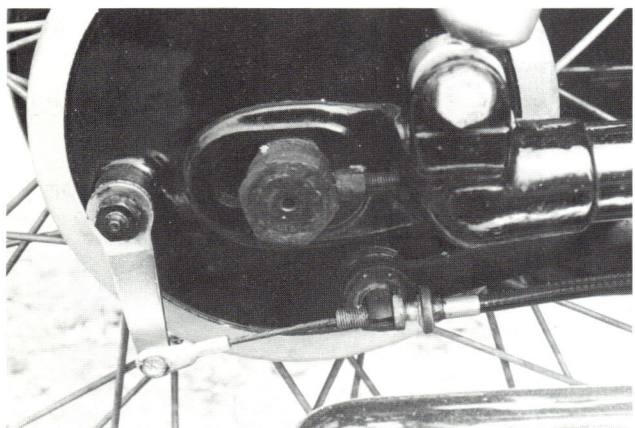
37

38

39

40

35. Cigar-shaped silencers have universal slotted mountings to accept a small triangular bracket which in turn is held by the pillion footrest. The stop lamp switch is missing although the brake lever does show a small lug for the switch return spring. The brake lever passing under the footrest is clamped to a cross-over shaft that runs through the swinging arm pivot.

36. The fully-enclosed chainguard was an excellent fitting that greatly improved rear chain life. The guard has two rubber blanking plugs. Removal of the rear plug will give access to four wheel hub nuts for wheel removal. The forward plug is for chain inspection. The large nut secures the sprocket and does not need to be disturbed unless for chain tensioning.

37. The large nut on the brake drum side is attached to the wheel spindle, removal of which will allow the rear wheel to be taken out after the four hub nuts, brake cable and hub tie have been uncoupled. Chain adjustment is by drawbolts screwed into the frame. Note the hub brake lever on this machine pointing downwards; this aligns with the position of the brake cable lug welded to the frame.

38. This rear brake cable lever is connected to the cross-over shaft. On some frames the cable lug is angled differently to necessitate a revised cable route and an upwards pointing hub brake lever. An hexagonal head screw was originally fitted.

39. A Lucas type 564 number plate and rear lamp unit was fitted to most BSA models at the time. The rear lens/reflector is located with two screws and the 6 volt 6/18W twin filament bulb has an offset pin bayonet fixing.

40. The adjustable three-position Girling shock absorbers have Silentbloc bushes pressed into their eyes. The outer black-painted and inner chrome-plated covers can be taken off if uprated springs are required.

Super Profile

41. The dual seat is held down by just two nuts located underneath and a bayonet bracket at the seat nose. White piping is correct for the year. Earlier seats had a more pronounced stepped shape.

42. Various types of transfer adorned the model range from time to time. As well as this piled arms decal the A10 Golden Flash had its own 'BSA Golden Flash' transfer applied to the rear mudguard beneath the number plate. Anomalies with transfers abound; at least they tastefully added the finishing touches.

43. From 1960 on, the air lever occupied a position on the frame near the seat nose. This allowed a very short cable run to the carburettor.

44. The triangular tool box has a hinged outer cover held by a single Dzus fastener. A Lucas RS108 voltage regulator is housed inside it. Every model that left the works had its own fifteen piece toolkit snugly wrapped up inside the box!

45. The famous BSA 'piled arms' transfer was attached to the toolbox and oiltank. This particular transfer is a pattern type distinguished by having a red outer belt and a yellow inner. Original design transfers have recently become available once more; the outer belt is more of a pink colour with a cream inner area. Prior to 1958, the upper lettering stated 'BSA Cycles Ltd'.

43

Super Profile

46.

47.

48.

49.

46. Throughout the history of the A10, there were a number of tank badges fitted. The pear-shaped badges appeared in 1959 and were complemented with these small triangular knee grips.

47. A 1956 A7 Shooting Star in its semi-sports trim, characterised by the front mudguard with minimal valancing. The fuel tank holds 4 Imp gallons and the star-type badge was an A7SS hallmark.

48. The A7SS was capable of achieving 95mph with an average fuel consumption return of 74mph. It could reach 77mph for a quarter mile standing start in just 16 seconds.

49. All A7 and A10 models had 19 inch diameter wheels using WM2 rims. Alloy full-width hubs were predominantly used for the 1956-57 seasons. The brake drums are 7 inch diameter with $1\frac{1}{8}$ inch wide shoes.

Super Profile

50.

51.

52.

53.

54.

50. With the arrival of swinging arm frames in 1954 came a welcome improvement in handling. However, the bikes were somewhat heavier. The A7SS weighed 416 lbs dry as against 382 lbs for its plunger-framed A7 Star Twin predecessor.

51. The pre-1958 swinging arm models are distinguished by having a cowled headlamp and flat sided toolbox and oiltank. The centre-stand was also modified for the 1958 season.

52. The BSA parallel twins had a sleek profile. Overall width for this model is 28 inches. The rear carrier is a contemporary accessory that was available through BSA Group dealers.

53. The dual seat was also revised in late 1957, so too was the rear mudguard stay arrangement. The pre-1958 models have a separate bracket linking the stay and the shock absorber mounting. The chromed bolt shown on the shock absorber mounting lug locates the oil tank through a pair of anti-vibration rubber bushes.

54. Many 1953-57 BSA models had this pressed steel headlamp cowling combined with fork spring shrouds. The headlamp is a Lucas model SS700P with a twin filament pre-focus bulb.

Super Profile

55

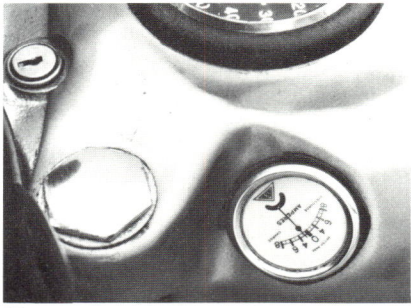

56

55. The Smiths Chronometric speedometer was a reliable instrument. It works on a clockwork mechanism principle, hence the apparent ticking motion of the needle! They can be dismantled quite easily, but this is best left to the experts, some of which are listed in the current classic motorcycle press. Note, on these earlier cowls, the lighting switch is on the left, with the ammeter positioned to the right.

56. For 1956, a Lucas type CZU27 ammeter was listed. They were susceptible to vibration and had a relatively short life span, hence the pattern type fitted here. At least it's British! The steering lock was a new feature for 1956.

57

57. This rear hub has a rather strange linkage. Normally, the hub brake lever was shorter, with the cable lug facing the cable in a horizontal position. The alloy full width hubs were to an Ariel design. The rear hub has a QD arrangement utilising a detachable spindle, knock-out spacer and four car type hub nuts taken out from the sprocket side. The brake cable and hub tie have also to be undone.

58. From its introduction in 1956, the fully-enclosed chainguard was a superb and efficient feature, giving the machine an uncluttered appearance. The guard is painted in the machine's base colour. From 1958, all guards were painted black. The cigar shaped exhaust silencer is a later design. 1956 versions had a parallel and longer expansion chamber that was slightly upswept.

59. Generally, the Girling rear units gave a lifetime's trouble-free service. They featured three-position adjustment that suited most tastes. The toolkit included a special C spanner for this purpose.

58

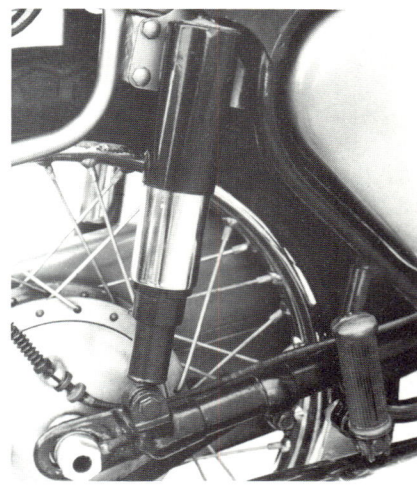

59

Super Profile

60. Earlier rear number plates had this contoured profile. It was to accept a separate reflector. The rear carrier, always finished in black, was a must for riders intent on serious touring.

61. A folding kickstart lever was another sporty feature. Quite a lot of work can be carried out on the gearbox with it still in the frame. A whole range of wide and narrow gear clusters could be fitted, if desired.

62. Notice how the front alloy full-width hub has a single pinch bolt to secure the spindle. Therefore the bottom fork legs will not accept the later cast-iron brake. Also, the spokes are bent into the hub in a reverse sequence.

63. Cable adjustment is provided at the hub with a ball-ended inner cable located in the hub brake lever. A grease nipple is provided for the lever mechanism. From this side, loosening of the large nut will enable the wheel spindle to be drawn out.

64. Handlebar fittings could vary depending upon year and model. This horn push is ideally situated. For 1956 the air lever was positioned on the handlebar as shown.

65. The first alloy cylinder heads had a bolted-on inlet manifold but it was later modified to be integral with the head, as shown here. The rocker gear oil feed banjo couplings can also be seen. They should be seated on a copper washer to avoid leakage. Note the special extended nuts to fasten the rocker box inspection caps. The horn used on the swinging arm models up to 1958 was a Lucas HF1234, after which a type HF1441 was specified.

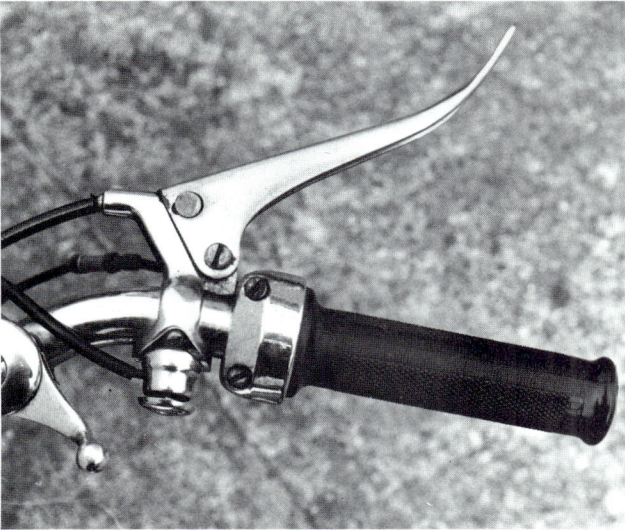

Super Profile

66

67

68

69

66. An experienced eye could tell an A7 engine at a glance with its slightly lower profile. At the top of the rocker box, the top engine steady can be seen. Many a shaky engine could be traced to a loose or even missing head steady. It consists of a couple of pressed steel brackets that go together to form a lug to accept a short tie rod.

67. This chaincase is probably from a later machine. The slotted cap was introduced from 1958 to enable easier clutch spring adjustment. The socket head cap screws are not original but make life easier for routine servicing. The three screws at the front are larger $\frac{5}{16}$ inch size and they go through the inner chaincase and spacer ring to locate into the engine crankcase.

68. Engine numbers can reveal all! All swinging arm A7s were stamped CA7; there was never a DA series. The SS stands for Shooting Star whilst the HC stamped underneath confirms high compression pistons have been fitted.

69. The A7 Shooting Star enjoyed this attractive circular 'star' badge. It was first fitted to the final plunger-framed A7 Star Twins. By about 1960 pear-shaped badges were applied to all twins, except the A10 Rocket Gold Star.

70

70. All tanks that featured circular badges, be they 'star' or 'piled arms' types, also had this larger version knee grip with the block characters BSA. The winged B motif was first used by BSA in 1946, the year in which the first A7 was introduced.

Super Profile

C1. Probably the most handsome model of the A7 and A10 range was the A7 Shooting Star. This superb 1956 example is owned by Bert Smith of Easton, Nr. Wells, Somerset. The A7SS is particularly remembered for its duo-tone green finish, dark bottle green for the frame and light polychromatic green for the fittings.

C2. Apart from the colour scheme, the A7SS differed from the standard A7 by having an alloy cylinder head, sports cam and other tuning features.

Super Profile

C3. The 1954-57 styling was highlighted by the headlamp cowl, flat-sided tool box and matching oil tank. The alloy full-width hubs were used for 1956 and 1957. This machine has a fully enclosed rear chain cover. Although it was an optional feature for the A7, the Shooting Star had this equipment as a standard fitting.

C4. The A7SS and other sports derivatives had a shallow front mudguard either painted or, later on, chromed. Note the centre-stand; on the earlier swinging arm models it had a tendency to touch down too early, making the operation a very strenuous exercise!

Super Profile

C5

C6

C7

C5. The alloy cylinder head was pioneered by some Daytona-winning A7 Star Twins in 1954. It then appeared on the swinging arm A7SS. In 1956 it was redesigned as shown on this machine, where the manifold is part of the casting. Previously, the manifold was bolted to the head.

C6. The pressed-steel cowl allowed the headlamp to have some vertical adjustment; note the rubber beading at the headlamp joint. The tank has a gold line at the chrome panel border. The silver star badge was a hallmark for the A7SS.

C7. Experienced A7/A10 riders reckoned the A7SS power unit to be the best all-rounder. It was free revving, exhilarating at speed yet it proved to be docile and well mannered in town. The pre-1958 flat-sided oil tank can be seen.

Super Profile

C8. One of the most persistent oil leaks was at the rocker box to cylinder head joint. Many owners, especially of alloy cylinder head models, omit the paper gasket and use a proprietary jointing cement. The outer timing cover was originally located with slotted head screws. The socket cap head screws, however, are far superior being easier to take out and they give a tighter fastening.

C9. The carburettor drip tray was a common feature ever since the first A7 of 1946. With the magneto lying beneath the float chamber only the foolhardy would omit this item! The A7SS did not have an air-cleaner as standard equipment, but instead, the chromed bellmouth fitted to the carb intake has always been the more popular feature.

C10. One of BSA's most thorough and proven designs, the A7 Shooting Star. Throughout the 1950s it symbolised stability and invincibility, not just for BSA, but for the whole British motorcycle industry.

Super Profile

C11

C12

C13

C11. This excellent 1960 A10 Golden Flash is owned by Ken Nelson of Three Legged Cross, Dorset. This is the basic 650cc model in its final form. Alternative colour schemes for that year were sapphire blue or black. From 1958, all frames and forks were painted black.

C12. The overall styling with a nacelle type of headlamp mounting dates from 1958. It was a common format then being used by BSA for nearly all their models, including the D7 Bantam. It was also later carried on by the A50 and A65 unit twins.

C13. The wheel hubs are correctly painted black, with a chrome or polished outer band. The brakes are a cast-iron, full width hub type. This particular machine has a fully enclosed rear chain cover. It was an optional but very useful piece of equipment.

Super Profile

C14. Viewed from the front, the exhaust pipes have a graceful curve. Note how the drive side pipe has a small bend near the footrest to line up with the silencer. The timing side pipe runs straight.

C15. The swinging arm engines had generous cooling fins. Even the exhaust clamp rings have ample finning. Not only do they serve as a decorative feature but can prevent blueing of the exhaust pipe.

C16. The alloy primary chaincase has a number of apertures. The upper inspection cap was a feature given to all models since 1946. The slotted cap was introduced in 1958 when BSA revised the method of clutch adjustment. Underneath the chaincase, but obscured by the exhaust pipe, an oil drain plug incorporating an oil level standpipe was fitted from 1960. The 'dome' cast into the chaincase is to allow for a transmission shock absorber.

Super Profile

C17

C18

C17. The slim valanced mudguards were a 1960 onwards feature. Sports versions had the option of chromed mudguards with no side valancing. The 'roll-on' centre stand was redesigned in 1958. The extension pedal has a small rubber pad pushed over the end.

C18. The power unit has excellent eye appeal. The elliptical gearbox slots in well with the 3-lobed outer timing cover. The footrest and gearchange pedals are mounted upon serrated shafts enabling adjustment to suit individual taste.

Super Profile

C19. The pear-shaped plastic tank badges were first used by BSA in 1958 for the 250cc ohv C15. They were gradually introduced to the twins from then on. They are each retained by a single screw and have an anti-vibration rubber backing. The red lining at the chrome panel border is perhaps just a little heavy. Note the small rubber knee grips compared to those of the A7SS model.

C20. By 1960 it was difficult to tell A7 and A10 models apart. Even the A7SS had identical styling such as this. Apart from the engine number coding you could tell the difference by counting the cylinder barrel fins. There were 7 for the A7 and 8 for the A10. (The cast-iron cylinder head for both the A7 and A10 models has 4 horizontal fins).